Our Lady of Guadalupe
And the Conquest of Darkness

ISBN 0-931888-12-3

Our Lady of Guadalupe
And the Conquest of Darkness

Warren H. Carroll

Christendom Press
134 Christendom Dr.
Front Royal, Virginia 22630

DEDICATION

To the holy memory of
Most Reverend RAYMOND A. LANE,
son of Massachusetts,
missionary bishop in China,
who introduced me to the tender love of the Mother of God
and the privilege and glory of devotion to her
and especially to her Most Holy Rosary,
who gave me the rosary I still carry,
this little book in honor of the Blessed Virgin Mary
and her brave sons who conquered Mexico for Christ
is dedicated with profound and lasting gratitude.

Contents

1.
More Than a World Apart
(1487)

Once there was a world within the world, self-contained, complete within itself. On its every side were impassable barriers made by the gods: to the north an utter desert which that world called Mictlan, dead man's land, where one can traverse sun-blasted miles without seeing a single living thing; to the east and west the endless sea; to the south sodden, almost impenetrable jungle, the domain of Tlaloc the rain god. Like a cup held in these iron hands were the good lands, where the tall corn waved green and gold, bright flowers bloomed, and lakes shimmered in the sun. Some twenty million people lived there. Almost fifteen million of them were ruled by the empire of the Mexica (who came, much later, to be known to historical writers as Aztecs) with their capital at an island city with a population of three hundred thousand or more: Tenochtitlan, Cactus Rock, where salt Lake Texcoco and fresh Lake Chalco joined.

They had reached the first stage of civilization, which is cities and writing, though their writing was still in the process of development out of pictures. They were in touch, although distantly, with the somewhat older civilization of the Mayas at the edge of the southern jungles. Oddly enough, they had never invented the wheel; but they used human porters very efficiently, and their city built on water was an engineering marvel. There was no apparent, external reason why they should not have been growing as other civilizations like them grew, from ancient Mesopotamia and China to classical Greece and Rome: seeking truth and justice, honoring virtue even when not practicing it, questing for the divine.

But this self-contained, isolated world had taken a very different course.

The Aztecs, like the Mayas, counted by twenties. Each of their months had twenty days, making eighteen of them in a year, with five days left over. Each twenty-day month had its festival dedicated to one of their gods. Most of these festivals were marked by sacrifices, ranging from one to thousands. The sacrifices were of people–usually adult men, but fairly often children as well.

Every Aztec city and large town had a central square, from which a high pyramidal temple rose, and four gates opening upon four roads approaching the town in straight lines extending at least five miles, each ending at one side of the temple pyramid. On each side of the temple pyramid was a steep stairway to its top. The whole structure was skillfully tapered inward, suggesting even greater height than the 90 to 100 feet that was common. Month after month, year after year, in temple after temple, the sacrificial victims came down the roads to the steps, climbed up the steps to the platform at the top, and there were bent backwards over large convex slabs of polished stone by a hook around the neck wielded by a priest with head and arms stained black, never-cut black hair all caked and matted with dried blood, and once-white garments soaked and stained with innumerable gouts of crimson. An immense knife with a blade of midnight black volcanic glass rose and fell, butting the victim open. His heart was torn out while still beating and held up for all to see, while his ravaged body was kicked over the edge of the temple platform where it bounced and slithered in obscene contortions down the steps to the bottom a hundred feet below. Later, the limbs of the body were eaten.

Many primitive peoples have practiced occasional human sacrifice and some have practiced cannibalism. None has ever done so on a scale remotely approaching that of the Aztecs. No one will ever know how many they sacrificed; but the law of the empire required a thousand sacrifices to the Aztec tribal god Huitzilopchtli in every town with a temple, every year; and there were 371 subject towns in the Aztec empire, though not all of them had full-scale temples. There were many other sacrifices as well. The total number was at least 50,000 a year, probably much more. The early Mexican historian Ixtlilxochitl estimated that one out of every five children in Mexico was sacrificed. It is known that entire tribes, numbering in the tens of thousand, were on several occasions exterminated by sacrifice.

Two chief gods of the Aztec pantheon, to which most of the sacrifices were made, were the Aztecs' own god Huitzilopochtli, the Hummingbird Wizard, called Lover of Hearts and Drinker of Blood, and the principal deity of Mexico, Tezcatlipoca, demiurge of creation. "He Who Is at the Shoulder" as the tempter. An almost universal symbol in Mexican religions was the serpent. Sacrifices were heralded by the prolonged beating of an immense drum made of the skins of huge snakes, which could be heard two miles away.

Nowhere else in human history has Satan so formalized and institutionalized his worship with so many of his own actual titles and symbols.

There was a human creator of this nightmare as well, a man who long remained in history's shadows, only recently emerging in his full stature from continuing research on the Aztecs, one of the most terrifying figures ever to stalk among men: Tlacaellel. The native annalist Chimalpahin Quauhtlehuanitzin summarized his career as follows:

> There were many great kings who inspired fear far and wide, but the one who was the most courageous, the most illustrious in the state, was the great captain, the great warrior Tlacaellel.... It was he who established the worship of the devil Huitzilopochtli, the god of the Mexicans.[1]

Tlacaellel was the architect of the Aztec empire. He developed and carried out the plan of cementing that empire by a regular tribute of victims for human sacrifice, and by requiring that *all* Mexican nobility attend the great sacrifices, and that *all* Mexican warriors take prisoner deliberately for sacrifice. For this purpose he invented the "Flower Wars," fake conflicts among allies whose sole purpose was to obtain sacrificial victims who would be, for Huitzilopochtli, "like bread hot from the griddle, soft and delicious."[2] Tlacaellel's answer to every military reverse and natural calamity—there was a series of climatic disasters from 1451 to 1454–was greatly to increase the number of sacrificial victims.

Tlacaellel was born in the same year as the first emperor Montezuma, 1398. He emerged as a leader through success in war at the age of thirty-one, in 1429. He remained the power behind the throne for the rest of his life. Passed over for emperor in 1440 in favor of Montezuma I in a last spasm of resistance to his developing policy of rule by mass human sacrifice (through Montezuma supported it as well), Tlacaellel picked the next three emperors while declining the throne himself because, as he said, "I am already king."[3] He lived to be ninety years old and effectively ruled the Aztec empire for sixty-seven years.

The climax of Tlacaellel's macabre life came in 1487 when he was eighty-nine years old. The occasion was the dedication of the immense new pyramid-temple of Huitzilopochtli in the center of Tenochtitlan (Cactus Rock, later Mexico City)–five stories and over 100 feet high with 114 steps to the top, honeycombed with apartments, corridors and shrines where several thousand of the bloodstained priests lived, the center of a complex 70 buildings enclosed by the richly decorated *Coatepantli*, the Serpent Wall. Tlacaellel decided that this central temple should be dedicated with the greatest mass sacrifice of his fifty-eight years of dominance in the Aztec empire. As always, he had his way. In R.C. Padden's memorable description:

> Well before daybreak of the opening day, legionnaires prepared the victims, who were put in close single file down the steps of the great pyramid, through the city, out over the causeways, and as far as the eye could see. For the average person viewing the spectacle from his roof top, it would appear that the victims stretched in lines to the ends of the earth. The bulk of the unfortunates were from hostile provinces and the swollen tanks of slavery. On the

pyramid's summit four slabs had been set up, one at the head of each staircase, for Tlacaellel and the three kings of the Triple Alliance, all of whom were to begin the affair as sacrificial priests. All were in readiness; the lines of victims were strung out for miles, with great reservoirs at their ends, thousand of trapped humans milling about like cattle, awaiting their turn in the line that was about to move. Suddenly, the brilliantly arrayed kings appeared on the platform and silence fell over the city. Together they approached Huitzilopochtli's chapel and made reverent obeisance. As they turned to join their aides at the four slabs, great snakeskin drums began to throb, announcing that the lines could now begin to move.[4]

Relays of priests despatched the victims. As each group tired, others of the thousands who were to live below in the new temple stepped forward to relieve them and keep up the pace. Years of practice had given them a skill and speed almost incredible. Reliable evidence indicates that it took only fifteen seconds to kill each victim. Blood and bodies cascaded in an endless stream down the temple steps. Hearts were assembled in piles and skulls in racks.

It went on for *four days and four nights*. More than *eighty thousand men* were killed. Tlacaellel had commanded all the high nobility of Mexico to be present, watching from scented, rose-covered boxes; but eventually the bonds of custom and even of fear were burst by overwhelming horror, and most of the spectators fled. Along with many of the people of the city. Even those who could hide from the sight of what was happening were unable any longer to endure the stench.

But Tlacaellel at eighty-nine remained to the very end, watching the victims killed at fifteen seconds per man, until the last of the eighty thousand had their hearts torn out before his devouring eyes.

It would be a hardy soul who would undertake to make a catalogue of all the horrors of history, and try to make many comparisons among them. But still, no scene after the Passion of Christ would seem to have quite so good a claim to be the worst of all, as this one in Mexico City in the year 1487.

In this year in the town of Cusuhtitlan, on the shore of salt Lake Texcoco twelve miles north of Cactus Rock, there lived a boy of thirteen who had probably already begun to learn the trade of maker of reed mats by which he was later to earn his living. He was probably one of the *macehualtin*, the despised poor of the Aztec empire, rather than one of the nobly born *Pipiltin*, "sons of lords," who by Tlacaellel's command had to witness the sacrifice. We may presume he stayed far away from it, though perhaps with the natural curiosity and relative insensitivity to the impact of suffering and death which are characteristic of thirteen-year-old boys, he might have gone close enough at some point for a quick look. His name was Cuauhtlatohuac, "he who talks like an eagle." (An eagle perched on a cactus growing out of a rock, with a snake in its beak, was the symbol of Aztec Tenochtitlan, Cactus Rock.) Approximately forty years later, Cuauhtlatohuac was to be baptized with the Christian name of Juan Diego; and it was to him that the Mother of God, Our Lady of Guadalupe, appeared.

But the Blessed Virgin Mary, Mother of the Church, does not act alone. She has sons, and she has daughters, who also have their part to play in the achievement of good and the destruction of evil.

Within the sharply limited world of Mexico in 1487 no possible source of rescue could be seen. Christianity had never been preached. The victimized people did not know to Whom to pray for help. Their lifelong training and orientation was to believe Tlacaellel's system to be not only the right one, but the only one. (Because of his very great age, few men in Mexico City in 1487 could have remembered anything of a Mexico Tlacaellel did not rule.) Theirs was a voiceless cry, voiceless even in the language of the spirit—a dumb agony, a rending pain without remedy that cried out to Heaven for the vengeance that is the Lord's, and the rescue that can be man's.

Eastward, toward the sunrise, rolled the ocean.

River Oceanus, the Greeks had called it, the waters that ring the inhabited world. The Ocean Sea, men called it in 1487, when Portuguese Bartholomew Dias was rounding the Cape of Good Hope, and Madeira and the Canaries and even the Azores well out into its blue-gray expanses had been discovered and settled. No man had crossed the Ocean Sea from near shore to far shore, only the Vikings island-hopping in the subarctic seas, mainly in search of timber, their voyages now forgotten. Most thought such a crossing impossible. Indeed, had America not been there, for the ship of Europe in 1487 it would have been impossible.

Across that portion of the Ocean Sea now called the Atlantic in 1487, the year of the ghastly mass sacrifice to dedicate the temple of Huitzilopochtli in Cactus Rock, upon a dry and rocky peninsula jutting out like a mailed fist from the body of Christian Europe, dwelt a people more than a world apart from the domain of the Hummingbird Wizard. While the lords and common people of the Aztec empire were rigorously conditioned to think and act collectively rather than individually, their counterparts in Spain were exactly the opposite, individualists to the core. They freely yielded political obedience only to their king or queen, and then only if their traditional rights were respected. But almost all of them obeyed the Church, for they were a Christian and a Catholic people, whose Lord Jesus Christ had Himself been a Victim of the dark powers which ruled Tlacaellel's Mexico. While the men of the Aztec empire were held

15

in thrall by fear and horror, the Spaniards of this era were probably the most fearless nation history has ever known. For more than 770 years they had been locked in mortal combat with a relentless enemy–militant Islam–for the reconquest of their beloved country. With that heritage, now close to final triumph in that immense struggle, they had the best fighting men on earth.

For half a millennium towered Cordoba had been the Muslim capital of Spain. It was a Christian city now, reconquered by King St. Ferdinand, San Fernando; and in that city, in the spring of the year of horror in Mexico, 1487, reinforcements for the latest Christian army of reconquest were mustering. The main army under King Ferdinand the Catholic of Aragon was caught between two Muslim forces. Queen Isabel the Catholic of Castile, the wife of Ferdinand, had called up the reinforcements — every man able to bear arms in all Andalusia in the south of Spain, up to the age of seventy. She herself marshalled those who responded. It was Isabel, far more even than the bold Ferdinand, who had made the Spain that was about to burst the ancient bonds of Ocean and transform and girdle the world. She had unified Spain, bringing it justice, law and order; she had inspired it with a renewed awareness of its Catholic identity and mission; now she was about to complete the centuries-old task of its reconquest.

Isabel the Catholic is probably the greatest woman ruler in history. Born in Madrigal de las Altas Torres (Song of the High Towers) in Castile in 1451, she was thirty-six years old in 1487, at the height of her powers, nearing the summit of her career. She was adored by her people and especially by her soldiers, a golden-haired beauty with blue-green eyes who prayed the divine office every day like a nun, trusting in God for all things; who once rode two hundred miles without rest in a crisis (the last fifty at night in the rain), and tamed a rebel city with a word; who had borne and was raising five children, and knitted her husband's shirts herself; with love for her God and her people and her husband's and her children sparking like hearth-fire and her will like a Toledo blade.

The two never met; but Isabel of Song of the High Towers in Castile was more than a match for Tlacaellel of Cactus Rock.

The year before, a tall man with graying hair and a freckled face, Cristobal Colon, who signed himself in Latin Christopher Columbus, a master mariner for ten years and deeply knowledgeable in navigation and what was then known of geography, had come to Isabel and Ferdinand seeking their sponsorship for his project of sailing straight across the Ocean Sea from Spain to Asia. Isabel had warmed to him, as she so often did to men of honest dedication and genuine Christian faith–qualities she did much to inspire in everyone she met–but she was not sure of all the answers to the geographical questions raised by his proposed voyage, and in any case could not help him in the midst of the war to complete at last the long reconquest of Spain by regaining Granada from the Muslims. So Columbus was waiting for that war to end in triumph, as it finally was to do on January 2, 1492. After that, he hoped to undertake his westward voyage with Isabel's help and blessing.

In that same year of 1487, when the eighty thousand were torn apart in four days on the altar of the Hummingbird Wizard, two lived in Spain whose future was to be bound up in a far more intimate way with Mexico than the future of Queen Isabel or Columbus, neither of whom ever saw or learned of it, despite all they did which ultimately made its physical and spiritual conquest possible. One was a boy of nineteen from Vizcaya, the Basque province in the north of Spain, round-faced, solemn, resolute, devoted, probably beginning about then his Franciscan novitiate. His name was Juan de Zumarraga[2], and he would be bishop of Mexico for eighteen years, and the first to see the picture of Our Lady of Guadalupe.

The other was not yet even a boy, but a baby who had barely learned to walk and talk. His father, Martin Cortes de Monroy, was a poor squire in Extremadura, "Extremely Hard," the dry western province of Spain, magnificently described by Hilaire Belloc: "Those sweeps of the bare Iberian land, almost treeless, almost untenanted, resemble and recall the sea, but a sea upon a scale more than titanic, a sea moved by gales such as our world never knows."[5] Martin Cortes lived at Medellin, an out-of-the-way place on the Guadiana River about twenty miles east of ancient Merida, commanded—like so many towns in Spain, with their stormy history—by a frowning gray castle. The baby was sickly. The family chose St. Peter for his special patron, praying often to the Prince of the Apostles and the Rock of the Church to ask his intercession for the child, as he himself did also when he grew old enough to understand. The baby's name was Hernan, and he was to conquer Mexico for Christ and for Spain.

Part I
The Physical Conquest of Mexico

2.
The Shores of Nightmare
(1517-1519)

The expedition of Hernan Cortes was the third Spanish expedition to Mexico. He did not participate in either of the earlier two, but one of his later soldiers did, and he has left us the whole story as he saw it, written fifty years later in his old age, with incomparable simplicity, clarity, honesty, and vividness: Bernal Diaz del Castillo. He was not a polished writer; but as an eyewitness narrator of great events he is unsurpassed in world history. And Bernal Diaz speaks for more than himself–he speaks for the whole spirit and character of crusading Catholic Spain in the Age of Discovery. He was twelve years old when Queen Isabel died in 1504; his Spain was the Spain she made, and he was a man she would have perfectly understood and appreciated.

> I am Bernal Diaz del Castillo, a resident and magistrate of the most loyal city of Santiago de Guatemala, one of the discoverers and conquerors of New Spain (Mexico) and its provinces, native of the noble and distinguished town of Medina del Campo, son of Francisco Diaz del Castillo, who was magistrate there and known as The Gallant, and Maria Diaz Rejon, his legitimized wife, may they have glorious sainthood.
>
> I write for myself and for all my companions, the real conquerors, who served His Majesty in discovery, conquering, pacifying and colonizing New Spain, which is one of the best sections discovered in the New World, and this we did by our own efforts, without His Majesty knowing of it.
>
> With the help of God, I write the truth as I remember it, without flattering certain captains or putting down other. . . . God served to guard me from many dangers and from death and I give Him much thanks.[6]

Columbus' epochal discovery of 1492 and his settlement of Hispaniola beginning at the end of the following year had led to the rapid extension of Spanish exploration and colonization throughout much of the Caribbean, including the Caribbean coasts of Venezuela, Colombia and Panama. The island of Cuba was circumnavigated in 1508 and conquered and colonized in 1511 by Diego Velazquez, who had himself confirmed at court as its independent governor. Cortes accompanied Velazquez on his conquest, which was never really opposed, the Cuban Indians being very primitive, and served as his secretary and the royal treasurer. Bernal Diaz came to Cuba three years later. Three more years passed uneventfully except for a series of escapades by young Cortes (he was still in his twenties) with Catalina Juarez, whom he rather unwillingly married, and with the proud, ponderous and hot-tempered Governor Velazquez, who twice arrested him for sedition. Meanwhile, Isabel's grandson Charles, the future Holy Roman Emperor Charles V, became king of Spain at the beginning of 1516. Mexico remained undiscovered. Montezuma II was now ruling there. He heard faint, farfiltered rumors of the arrival of strangers in the east; but Mexico had no seafarers, and the reports had to pass through so many peoples, languages and cultures to reach Mexico from where the Spaniards were, that by the time they arrived they were little more than vague foreboding. The two worlds had not yet met.

On February 8, 1517 three ships and 110 men under Francisco Hernandez de Cordoba, with Anton de Alaminos of Palos, who had sailed with Columbus, their pilot, set out westward from a small port in Cuba, "having commended ourselves to God our Lord and to the Virgin St. Mary, our Lady, His blessed Mother," sailing west "towards our luck . . . knowing nothing about banks, nor currents, nor the winds which usually hold sway over those parts."[7] Traversing completely unknown waters for nine days, they arrived near Cape Catoche in the Yucatan peninsula. Yucatan was on the fringe of the Mexican culture area, inhabited by Mayan-speaking people preserving what had survived of the ancient Mayan civilization after a long decline. They were not under Aztec rule, but had adopted many of the Aztec religious customs including extensive human sacrifice. The Spaniards were ambushed the day after their landing. After repelling the attack, they saw their first small temples. "There were clay idols made of pottery," Bernal Diaz tells us, "with the faces of demons or women and other evil figures that showed Indians committing acts of sodomy with each other."[8] Continuing along the coast, upon landing again they were taken by the local Indians to temples covered with bas-reliefs of snakes. Bernal Diaz saw blood on the altars and on the long black hair of the priests. But these were only faint warnings of the actual extent of the evil gripping the land they had begun to approach.

At the next stop, after a storm, still on the Yucatan coast, the Spaniards were set upon while refilling their water casks. Francisco Hernandez de Cordoba received no less than ten wounds, and Bernal Diaz three. When they had finally retreated to the shore and their ships, fighting desperately for their lives, it was discovered that fully half their number had been slain. The survivors returned to Cuba, where their commander died of his wounds in a few days.

The first Christian reconnaissance of death's realm had ended in disaster, repulsed in its most outlying region, beyond the borders of Montezuma's empire.

The next year the Spaniards came back with twice the force—240 men in four ships. The fathers and the ancestors of these men for thirty generations had not won the longest war in history by being discouraged by a single reverse.

The second expedition to Mexico was led by Juan de Grijalba, a young kinsman of Governor Velazquez, rich and handsome, untypically gentle for a Spanish conquistador. Las Casas said of him: "He was of such natural condition that in point of obedience and even of humility and of other qualities, he would not have made a bad monk."[9] On Sunday, January 24, 1518 the Grijalba expedition heard the Mass of the Holy Spirit at Santiago de Cuba; they had their red, black and gold banners blessed, and set out to a fanfare of fife and drum. Coasting along Cuba and taking on stores, they did not reach Yucatan until May 4, when a brief landing was made at Cozumel island just offshore. On May 11 the commander missed one of his caravels (the magnificent little all-purpose vessel which had carried the Portuguese to India and Columbus back across the Atlantic through midwinter storms after his discovery of America and the wreck of his flagship, the *Santa Maria*); it had landed to pick up a pretty Indian girl who had been running along the coast for miles trying to attract the attention of its crew. She was from the island of Jamaica, already settled by Spaniards, so that some aboard could speak her language. She explained that she had been fishing with her husband and ten companions off the Jamaican coast, and had been carried to Yucatan by ocean currents. Her husband had been killed and their ten companions sacrificed on the altars of the devil-gods. She asked the Spaniards for rescue. Grijalba took her aboard as a messenger and interpreter.

Ten days later Grijalba and his men landed to plant Christ's standard by saying Mass before a pagan temple. They were attacked by the Yucatan Indians, very close to the place where Hernandez de Cordoba had been attacked, and probably by many of the same warriors who had defeated his expedition. Grijalba's force was almost as badly hurt; but with more men to cover their retreat, only seven soldiers were lost, though no less than sixty were wounded. Bernal Diaz remembered a homely detail about the fight.

> I recall that the skirmish took place where there were many locusts, which flew in our faces so that we sometimes mistook the arrows for locusts and did not shield ourselves, and so were wounded. At other times we thought the locusts were arrows, which greatly hampered our fighting.[10]

Grijalba sailed on, past the point where the Yucatan peninsula merges with the mainland do Mexico at Tabasco. There the Spaniards bartered with the Indians for gold trinkets. Asked where more could be obtained, the Indians said: "Mexico." It was the first time the Spaniards had heard the name.

They coasted northward. About the middle of June they came to several offshore islands, anchoring in the lee of the largest. Smoke was rising, but no people could be seen. The Spaniards landed. In the distance were snowcapped mountains. Before them were two houses of death, with the hideous faces of their gods grinning over altars where, the night before, five Indians had been killed, their hearts torn out, and their bodies dismembered. They very walls of the rooms with the altars were covered with human blood.

They were in the domain of Montezuma now, the empire Tlacaellel had built, ruled by Tezcatlipoca lord of darkness and Huitzilopochtli the Hummingbird Wizard. Their anchorage and the port behind it was later to be named Veracruz, the True Cross.

Montezuma, who was constantly informed of everything happening in or near his empire, had heard of the arrival, defeat and departure of Hernandez de Cordoba in Yucatan the year before, and had been following Grijalba's progress from the moment of his arrival. The situation was unprecedented in history: a sudden, direct, unexpected contact of two totally alien civilizations. But, on the Aztec side, much more was involved even than that, because of the legend of Quetzalcoatl.

Like most pagan legends, that of Quetzalcoatl among the Aztecs was fantastically convoluted, much of it beyond the power of human reason now to unravel since the Aztec civilization has perished utterly. Yet, because it so dramatically changed the course of history, this particular pagan legend has been the subject of almost as many different theories as there are writers on the subject. Crackpots and cultists to this day lay claim to Quetzalcoatl. He has been identified with everything and everyone from an interstellar intruder which became the planet Venus (Immanuel Velikovsky) to St. Brendan and Prince Madoc of Wales. In all probability he was none of the above. But the name seems at least to have been

21

associated with a very significant historical person. The most plausible candidate is a priest named Ce Acatl Topiltzin ("Our Prince, born in the year 1-Reed") of the Toltec nation that preceded the Aztec empire, and from which the Aztec nobility, the Pipiltin, claimed descent. Ce Acatl Topiltzin Quetzalcoatl was eventually driven out of central Mexico and crossed the Gulf of Campeche to the Yucatan peninsula where he was remembered and honored as the godlike leader Kukulcan.

Quetzalcoatl was one of the old gods; Topiltzin was his high priest and so took his name. But the chief god of the Toltecs was Tezcatlipoca, Smoking Mirror, lord of darkness, who demanded human sacrifice. Topilztin taught that the true God wanted no such thing; that He was of light, not darkness; that He wanted men to live, to serve Him, and to be chaste, not to be slain in His name.

Did Ce Acatl Topiltzin know—or did he simply hope? Only God knows. Tezcatlipoca and his adherents expelled Topiltzin, first from Tula, the Toltec capital, and then from Cholula. About the year 987 of the Christian era he crossed the sea to Yucatan and spent the rest of his life among the Mayas. But there was a prophecy that he would return from the eastern sea to reclaim what had been his and to resume the leadership of his people and their descendants. This prophecy was attributed to Ce Actl Topiltzin Quetzalcoatl himself. It dated his return to his name year, 1-Reed, which recurred only once every 52 years.

In the Mexican calendar, the year 1519 of the Christian era was a 1-Reed year.

While they continued to honor Quetzalcoatl as the deified Ce Acatl Topiltzin and preserved the memory of his kindness and charity and loathing of human sacrifice, at least from the time of Tlacaellel the Aztecs and their subject peoples made human sacrifices to him as well, though not so many as to Huitzilopochtli and Tezcatlipoca. They felt bound to such a total contradiction of his teaching because they regarded themselves as living in Tezcatlipoca's age, since he had driven Quetzalcoatl out; and in Tezcatlipoca's age, *all* gods must receive human sacrifices. But they also believed in the prophecy of Quetzalcoatl's return, and that when he returned, he would claim the kingdom of the Aztecs as its rightful ruler, banishing Tezcatlipoca and ushering in a new age.

As it happened, the prophecy was true . . . if Quetzalcoatl be read as the name given to Christ by a desperate people lost in darkness.

When Grijalba's ships lay at anchor in the roadstead of what was to be Veracruz, Montezuma finally sent his emissaries directly to them. Communication proved difficult because none among the strangers could speak Nahuatl, the language of the Aztecs, though they had two Indians with them who spoke Maya, which some of the Aztecs knew, and had picked up some Spanish. By this means the strangers told the chieftains of the embassy that they were not going to remain long, but would be back the next year. (Grijalba was under orders from Governor Velazquez to make no settlement yet.) Next year was the year 1-Reed.

The ambassadors came back with some ship's biscuit and some green beads the strangers had given them. Montezuma and the ten-man council of leaders of his realm, solemnly and fearfully debating the questions of what was happening to them, were inclined to believe these were Quetzalcoatl's men. In case they were, Montezuma put the biscuit in a golden chalice and enshrined it at Quetzalcoatl's temple in Tula. Yet the Hummingbird Wizard had to be propitiated too, so the beads were buried at the foot of his altar.

Still Montezuma was not sure. He could not understand why the god, or his party, had lost the ability to speak Nahuatl. Whether he thought the whole party immortal, since Quetzalcoatl had departed more than five hundred years before, is not clear. Montezuma was not thinking rationally at this point.

Indeed, the whole concept and realization of the return of Quetzalcoatl went deeper than reason. For no man, not even a Tlacaellel, can entirely efface the natural law God had written upon his heart. Those responsible for the gigantic horrors of the Mexican sacrifices could not have truly and always believed that such actions were right. Deep within them dwelt the fear–and sometimes, in their better moments, the hope–of a Savior who would also be an Avenger, who would stop the sacrifices, take the kingdom away from those who had inflicted them, and punish those responsible as, somewhere deep within themselves, however repressed, they knew that they deserved.

One word explains the paralysis of will, the agonized indecision of the absolute ruler of fifteen million people as he faced the forthcoming attack of a relative handful of Spaniards–the paralysis and indecision that the genius of Cortes divined, which made possible his astonishing victory.

That word is *guilt.*

It was all a bit too much for Juan de Grijalba, a man too cautious for greatness. He decided to sail back to Cuba. Before they left the Mexican coast, on the way to Yucatan, the Spaniards bartered for 600 polished axes with decorated wooden handles. Somehow they got the notion that these axes were made partly of gold. The unsinkable Bernal Diaz ends his account of the second expedition to the shores of nightmare with the wry comment:

> When the six hundred axes were brought out, they were all discolored like the copper they proved to be. This furnished a good laugh and great fun was made of our trading.[11]

It was a long way from the state of mind of Montezuma II and the ten-man council of the leaders of his realm.

Preparation for a third expedition had begun even before Grijalba returned. Despite his earlier clashes with Velazquez, Hernan Cortes was appointed to command it, largely through the influence of Velazquez's current secretary, Andres de Duero, "tall as an elbow, but wise and very silent, and he wrote well,"[12] and his accountant, Amador de Lares, an older man who had served 22 years in Italy where he was given a high post by Gonzalo de Cordoba, "the great captain," the finest soldier and one of the best men ever to serve Queen Isabel the Catholic, whom he followed devotedly almost all her life. So many Spaniards of this age were so much motivated by greed for gold that it is generally assumed that Andres de Duero and Amador de Lares, in making possible Cortes' appointment, were bought by bribes or promise. It is possible; there is some evidence of it in the case of Duero. But it is at least equally possible that they simply concluded, what the sequel proved so obviously true, that Cortes was by far the best man for the job. Their experience clearly gave them the basis on which to have made such a judgment.

Let us look a moment at Hernan Cortes, now thirty-three years old, as Bernal Diaz, who followed him to the very gates of Hell, describes him:

He was of a good height and body and well proportioned and of strong limbs and the color of his face was somewhat ashy and not very merry and had his face been longer he would have been handsomer, and his eyes had a somewhat loving glance yet grave withal, his beard was dark and sparse and short and . . . is chest was high and his back was of a good shape and he was lean and of little belly and somewhat bowlegged and his legs and thighs well set and he was a good horseman and skillful with all weapons on foot or on horseback and knew very well how to handle them, and above all a heart and a courage which is what matters. . . .[He wore] just a thin chain of gold of simple pattern and a trinket with the image of Our Lady the Virgin Saint Mary with her precious Son in her arms. . . . He prayed every morning with a [book of] Hours and heard Mass with devotion; he had for his protector the Virgin Mary our Lady (whom all Christians must hold as our intercessor and protector) as well as the Lord St. Peter and St. James and the Lord St. John the Baptist; and he was fond of giving alms. When he swore he said "on my conscience" and when his anger was aroused by some soldier, one of us, his friends, he said to him "may you live to rue it!" And . . . even at times when very angry he threw up a lament to heaven and he never said an ugly or offensive word to captan or soldier and he was most long suffering . . . and I always saw him in battle stepping in along with us. . . . He was a good cavalier and very devout to the Holy Virgin and to St. Paul and other saints. God pardon him his sins and me mine.[13]

Cortes had two banner standards made for the expedition, red and black with gold trim, with the royal arms of Spain and a cross on each side, with the words: "Brothers and companions, let us follow the sign of the Cross with true faith and in it we shall conquer."[14]

It had been the Emperor Constantine's slogan, flashed to him in the sky, when he went forth for the founding of Christendom upon what had been the pagan empire of Rome. Cortes was going forth under that same sign to found a Christian order upon what was the Satanic empire of the Aztecs.

Cortes departed from Santiago de Cuba on November 18, 1518, over the last-minute objections of Governor Velazquez, who had begun to realize that this was a man he could never really govern. At Trinidad on the south coast of Cuba, Cortes recruited most of Grijalba's just-returned men, including Bernal Diaz; then he picked up more men and supplies in Havana. In February 1519 he crossed to the island of Cozumel off Yucatan. Here he mustered his force: eleven ships, 508 Spanish soldiers, 100 sailors, just 16 horses (rare and very valuable in the New World, since the horse was not native to the Americas and only a comparative few had yet been imported and bred), 32 crossbows, 13 muskets, and four falconets (a small cannon) along with a few slightly larger bronze cannon. As the motto on his standards clearly indicated, Cortes' purpose from the beginning was conquest. With his tiny army he proposed to vanquish the Aztec empire.

The question of what right the Spaniards had to conquer the Indian people of the Americas was widely debated at the time in Spain and is still discussed, though the tendency now is automatically to assume that the conquest was wrong. But the Spaniards on the scene did not then concern themselves with it. For the unreflective, the 800-year tradition of the reconquest of Spain was enough, the tradition of the just was against the infidel invaders and occupiers of their homeland. Infidels were the same all over the world. But all the world was not the Spanish homeland.

But even the most reflective did not raise the issue for Mexico— except, later, for Las Casas, who became so much an advocate of all the Indians that he tried to pretend that the horrors of human sacrifice in Mexico were only a tiny fraction of what they actually were. For those who recognized the full reality of those horrors, they were enough. There can never be an obligation to stand by while thousands of innocent people are killed because of state or "religious" policy, if one has the power and the means to prevent it without causing still greater evils.

While at Cozumel, Cortes located a man who was to be indispensable to his entire vast undertaking: Jeronimo de Aguilar, a Spaniard who had taken minor orders and aspired to the priesthood, but had gone to America, been shipwrecked on Yucatan eight years before, and kept there ever since as a slave. He had kept his faith, his loyalty and his chastity, and accepted Cortes' invitation to join his expedition. After eight years among the Mayas Aguilar spoke their language almost perfectly. Cortes would not have to depend, as Grijalba had depended, on Indian interpreters who did not really understand what he was saying to them in Spanish, especially about the Christian faith.

Going on to Tabasco, Cortes fought a battle at Cintla in that region on March 25. The Indian attackers, though relatively primitive in their arms and tactics, outnumbered the Spaniards three hundred to one. Seventy Spaniards were wounded, but 200 Indians were killed and victory achieved. The beaten Indians sought to wipe out the memory of their attack with gifts, among them a girl of eighteen or nineteen, "of good appearance, intelligent, poised,"[15] whom the Spanish christened Marina when she was baptized soon afterward. They called her Dona Marina, Lady Marina, for her mother had been one of the Pipiltin, the Aztec aristocracy, but her stepfather had disliked her and therefore had given her to the Tabascoans beyond the imperial frontier. Marina neither felt nor owed any loyalty to those who had cast her out. She hesitated not a moment in accepting the strangers' cause as her own. Brought up in the highest Aztec circles, she spoke perfect Nahuatl; having lived for several years among the Tabascoans, she spoke their Maya dialect fluently; acutely intelligent and perceptive, she quickly picked up excellent Spanish. Nevertheless it was thought better on all formal occasions to have the translating into and out of Spanish done by Aguilar, who turned it into Maya, whereupon Marina turned it into Nahuatl. It was probably the most unusual and challenging task of simultaneous translation and linguistic interpretation ever undertaken, given the lack of any previous contact between Spanish and these two new languages, the difficulty of the concepts Cortes was attempting to express, and the gulf between the two civilizations. It went on all through the two and a half years of the conquest, which both Marina and Aguilar survived. Nowhere was Cortes more fortunate than in acquiring the devoted services of this alert, quick-witted Indian girl.

It was Holy Week of the Year of Our Lord 1519 for Christians, and the year 1-Reed for the Aztecs, when Cortes reached the island roadstead where Grijalba had anchored, from which the snowy peaks guarding the road to Mexico City could be clearly seen. On Holy Thursday, April 21 the anchor chains of Cortes' eleven ships clattered through hawseholes. Within half an hour the first Indians had arrived, bringing greetings from Montezuma and his local governor, Teuhtile. From them Cortes learned that he was on the shores of a tightly organized empire, of which Grijalba's expedition had provided only half-understood glimpses. As a farsighted man, he must have seen at once a substantial part of both the danger and the opportunity.

Cortes landed the next day, Good Friday. He planted his standards, heard Mass, and brought ashore the horses and the cannon, which were appropriately stationed. A camp was quickly built for the soldiers. The men from the lands beyond the sunrise had come to stay.

The wise men of Mexico had expected that the returning Quetzalcoatl would land not only in his name-year, 1-Reed, but also on his personal name day, called in their calendar 9-Wind. Good Friday, April 22, 1519, was a 9-Wind day in the 1-Reed year. As a priest, Ce Acatl Topiltzin Quetzalcoatl wore black. Cortes, landing this day, was dressed in black for the commemoration of Good Friday.

As with Grijalba the year before, Montezuma had followed every step of Cortes' progress. Surviving Aztec records tell us how he responded.

> This is what he felt in his heart: *He has appeared! He has come back! He will come here, to the place of his throne and canopy, for that is what he promised when he departed!*
>
> Motecuhzoma [Montezuma] sent five messengers to greet the strangers and to bring them gifts. . . . He said to them: "Come forward, my Jaguar Knights, come forward. It is said that our lord has returned to this land. Go to meet him. Go to hear him. Listen well to what he tells you; listen and remember.". . . .
>
> While the messengers were away, Motecuhzoma could neither sleep nor eat, and no one could speak with him. He thought that everything he did was in vain, and he sighed almost every moment. He was lost in despair, in the deepest gloom and sorrow. Nothing could comfort him, nothing could claim him, nothing could give him any pleasure.
>
> He said: "What will happen to us? Who will outlive it? Ah, in other times I was contented, but now I have death in my heart! My heart burns and suffers. . . . But will our lord come here?"[16]

On Easter Sunday Cortes took Montezuma's emissaries to Easter High Mass, chanted by father Bartolome de Olmedo, the able and faithful chaplain of his expedition (who, Bernal Dias tells us, had a very fine voice). Dining with them later, on shipboard, Cortes explained his mission: he represented a great ruler across the sea (King Charles, soon to be Emperor

Charles V), who wished friendship and trade with Montezuma, and had sent Cortes to penetrate his domain.

Could Quetzalcoatl speak this? He might, for there remained behind all the hellish excrescences of the Mexican pantheon the concept of an ultimate Ruler and Sustainer of the universe, remote but real: Ometecuhtli, Lord of Life, union of dualities, the god beyond the stars. Almost all pagan peoples have such a concept at the deepest wellsprings of their religious thought, for belief in God is natural to man, not dependent on revelation and grace as full Christianity is; and even the Aztec horrors had not effaced this belief in Mexico. In Cortes' description of Charles it is quite possible that the Aztec ambassadors thought they were hearing of Ometecuhtli.

There was another test to perform. Suddenly the emissaries sprinkled Cortes' Easter dinner, made from the presents of rich food they had brought to him, with a seasoning of human blood.

It was as though the bright spring sun had darkened. The Spaniards spat in disgust, turning away appalled from the polluted meal. Cortes called for chains and put them around the feet and necks of the emissaries. He ordered a cannon loaded with a maximum charge of powder. It went off with a searing flash, a mighty roar, and a pungent smell of sulfur. The emissaries collapsed in a faint. Cortes had them revived, probably none too gently. He knew now what he faced. It seems likely that an immense and righteous anger suddenly rose in him, so that he wanted to kill out of hand these men who regularly killed and ate their fellows and consumed their blood, like ghouls and vampires. But instead, in the chivalrous spirit of Christian knighthood, he formally challenged them to personal combat.

> I have heard that the Mexicans are very great warriors, very brave and terrible. If a Mexican is fighting alone, he knows how to retreat, turn back, rush forward and conquer, even if his opponents are ten or even twenty. But my heart is not convinced. I want to see it for myself. I want to find out if you are truly that strong and brave.[17]

He took off their chains, gave them Spanish swords and shields, and said: "It will take place very early, at daybreak. We are going to fight each other in pairs, and in this way we will learn the truth. We will see who falls to the ground!"[18]

The emissaries were overwhelmed. There were convinced now by his reaction to the human blood that he was indeed Quetzalcoatl, the enemy of human sacrifice:

Lord, we were not sent here for this by your deputy Motecuhzoma! We have come on an exclusive mission, to offer you rest and repose and to bring you presents. What the lord desires is not within our warrant![19]

With this they leaped into their canoes, paddling frantically for shore as though their lives depended on it. Those without paddles actually paddled with their hands, crying: "Captains, paddle with all your might! Faster, Faster! Nothing must happen to us here! Nothing must happen!"[20]

Montezuma had left word to be called instantly whenever his emissaries returned from the coast, whatever the hour of day or night. They came at eleven o'clock at night, having travelled their last hours in the darkness in view of the urgency of their message, though Aztecs had a mortal terror of the dark. Montezuma refused to receive them in his palace, but told them to go to the House of the Serpent. Before he heard a word from them, he painted two captives chalk-white and had them sacrificed, sprinkling the messengers with the blood from their torn-out hearts. He may have sacrificed them himself. Then he let the emissaries speak. It was like a report on the arrival of creatures from another planet:

They dress in iron and wear iron casques on their heads. Their swords are iron, their bows are iron, their shields are iron, their spears are iron. Their deer carry them on their backs wherever they wish to go. These deer, our lord, are as tall as the roof of a house.

The strangers' bodies are completely covered, so that only their faces can be seen. Their skin is white, as if it were made of lime. They have yellow hair, though some of them have black. Their beards are long and yellow, and their mustaches are also yellow. . . .

Their dogs are enormous, with flat ears and long, dangling tongues. The color of their eyes is a burning yellow; their eyes flash fire and shoot off sparks, their bellies are hollow, their flanks long and narrow. They are tireless and very powerful. They bound here and there, panting, with their tongues hanging out. And they are spotted like an ocelot.[21]

Our Aztec sources tell us that when Montezuma heard this report, it was as though his heart shrivelled up in his breast. He almost fainted with terror.

Convinced now that Cortes was Quetzalcoatl, Montezuma thought of flight; but in the virtual paralysis of his will, he could not even flee. Above all else he feared to meet the strangers face to face, so he set himself to try to discourage them from visiting him in Mexico City as Cortes had said he had come to do. He sent Cortes rich presents, including the serpentine turquoise mask of Quetzalcoatl and a round calendar of gold the size of a cartwheel; but the emissaries who brought them were ordered to urge the strangers not to come to Mexico City, and they were accompanied by magicians charged to prevent their further advance by spells, and even by a double of Cortes, whose probably induced illness was intended to infect him by magical means.

Cortes, with the image of "Our Lady the Virgin Saint Mary with her precious Son in her arms" around his neck, was unaffected.

It seems likely that it was this new group of emissaries–though it may have been earlier one, at Cortes' Easter dinner–which actually sacrificed several captives before the Spaniards' very eyes. (At fifteen seconds per man, it was hard to move fast enough to stop them.) In one of the most poignant moments in the Aztec records, they tell us that at the sight of the sacrifice, they saw tears rise in the eyes of these battle-hardened Spanish soldiers.

A few days later, it was the hour of the Angelus, observed in Cortes' army as throughout most of Christian Europe in that age by the ringing of a bell, whereupon all who heard it would at once drop to their knees in prayer, recalling the Annunciation and invoking Our Lady. Governor Teuhtile was present as the Spaniards knelt before a cross to pray the Angelus. He asked how they "could humiliate themselves before such a piece of wood made in such a manner."[22]

Cortes turned to Father Olmedo: "This is a good time, Father, for you to tell our holy faith."[23]

"He did," says Bernal Diaz, "and no theologian could have done better."[24]

> After he had explained how we were Christians and how our holy faith gave us the power to come here, he spoke of their wicked idols and how our sign of the cross came from the Passion and death of Our Lord in heaven and on earth, Jesus Christ, Who died to save humanity, to arise on the third day, and Who is now in Heaven, the true God, Whom we adore and in Whom we believe. He told them to do away with human sacrifices and not to rob each other or adore their evil idols.[25]

Soon afterward Montezuma ordered all of his Indians to withdraw from the neighborhood of the Spanish camp, cutting off what had been a regular supply of food to them. Bernal Diaz says that later the Spanish learned the reason. The Aztec emperor had consulted his gods, who told him most emphatically to listen no more to any talk about the Cross of Christ and the Mother of God. Bernal here names the two great gods. "Huitzilopochtli, god of war, he–like all the Spaniards with Cortes–called

"Huichilobos," an untranslatable Spanish pun inadequately rendered into English as "Witchywolves." Tezcatlipoca he calls, simply, the god of Hell.

But two of Montezuma's representatives, from the highest levels of the Aztec aristocracy, named Atonal and Tlamapanatzin, did not obey his command, but came forward to tell Cortes of a book about Quetzalcoatl's return that Montezuma had ordered burned, but that they had secreted. They offered to turn it over to Cortes if he would commit himself to the destruction of Montezuma' tyranny.

Cortes, already totally committed to that end, cheerfully promised it. He accepted the mysterious book, but seems to have told them it was not as important as they thought. What was really important was that, if they wished to serve him, they should become Christians. Atonal and Tlamapanatzin were baptized in late May of 1519.

At about the same time Cortes was contacted by the Totonac people of Cempoala, a province just up the coast only recently added to the Aztec empire and heavily burdened by its taxes and other impositions. They asked him to help them regain their freedom. Delighted by this development, he began making plans to use their nearby territory as a base for his planned march inland.

But first Cortes felt a need to regularize his position, as a good subject of King Charles. Technically, he was only in Mexico as leader of an expedition sent by the Governor of Cuba, who had told him not to settle there and moreover had revoked his commission just before his departure, though Cortes and his men had ignored that. King Charles had not really sent him, though Cortes intended that in good time the King should, in admiration and gratitude, confirm all his actions retrospectively (as indeed he did). Cortes knew that most of his men had no more wish than he to conquer an empire for the fat, unenterprising governor of Cuba. He shrewdly let them say so, in no uncertain terms, to Velazquez's partisans among them. The army then proceeded to constitute the expedition as a Spanish municipality, according to all the forms of Spanish laws, directly under the Crown, with Cortes as Captain-General and Chief Justice, and its own elected council, or *cabildo*. The municipality was their camp by the shore; and this was when they named it: Villa Rica do Vera Cruz, Rich Town of the True Cross. Cortes took possession of Mexico in the name of King Charles of Spain–who, unbeknownst to him, was about to be elected Holy Roman Emperor, the temporal heir and guardian of Christendom and Christendom's leader against the infidels.

Before visiting his new allies of Cempoala, Cortes sent Pedro de Alvarado, one of his principal subordinate officers, on a reconnaissance inland, to scout the country and obtain food, since the Indians were no longer supplying it. Alvarado was tall, red-haired, handsome and cheerful, very active and a fine horseman; the Mexicans nicknamed him Tonatiuh, "the Sun." Marching inland with a hundred men, he found that the people would leave every town before he arrived because of Montezuma's order of nonintercourse; and town after town held scenes of horror. Trunks of bodies lay scattered in the bloodstained temple rooms, the arms and legs having been taken away to eat; the sacrificial knives and stones were on display. Sunny Alvarado returned less merry than when he had set out.

Along the tropical coast with the blue sea and the white sand and its fringe of green-flaring palm trees to their right and the 18,000-foot snowcapped peak of Mount Orizaba, called in Nahuatl the Mountain of the Star, piercing the sky to their left, Cortes' five hundred marched north to Cempoala about the middle of June. In every town and village were the horrible signs of human sacrifice, such as Alavarado had seen on his reconnaissance.

The town of Cempoal welcomed them with flowers and feasting, its chief–an immensely fat man–apologizing profusely for being unable to give them richer presents or entertain them in even higher style because of the heavy taxes Cempoal had to pay to Cactus Rock. Cortes responded that he and his men served the great King Charles who had sent them "to punish evildoers, right the wrongs they had committed, and end the sacrifice of human souls."[26] The next day they marched on, accompanied now by Cempoalan porters, and set up their camp in an excellent defensive position at Quiauiztlan, just a few miles north of Cempoal. The fat chief came to them there to explain at much greater length how his people had suffered under Aztec rule. Among their exactions, he said, was a tribute of their sons and daughters and wives for sacrifice or slavery.

At almost that moment, five of Montezuma's tax collectors arrived. Cortes persuaded the Cempoalans to arrest them, thereby making them rebels against the Aztec empire; then he secretly released two of the tax collectors to carry a conciliatory message to Montezuma. The Cempoalans, realizing that the die was cast, swore allegiance to King Charles. Cortes began construction of a fort to protect his new base, on a plain near the shore, near Quiauiztlan. He joined personally in the construction work, carrying earth and stone on his back alongside his men.

On July 10 the council of Veracruz, Corte's town, sent a letter to King Charles informing him officially of all that they, his subjects, had done in this new land of Mexico, and of their full support for Hernan Cortes. They discussed at some length the "most horrid and abominable custom which truly ought to be punished and which until now we have seen in no other part [of the world], and this is that . . . in the presence of the idols they open their chests while they are still alive and take out their hearts and entrails and burn them before the idols, offering the smoke as

32

sacrifice. Some of us have seen this, and they say it is the most terrible and frightful thing they have ever witnessed."[27] Cortes also wrote a personal letter to King Charles, sent in the same ship with the letter of his town council, which most unfortunately has not survived. Of its contents we know only (from a reference in a later letter from Cortes to the King) that in it he told His Most Catholic Majesty about Montezuma and his empire and pledged that he "would take him alive in chains or make him subject to your Majesty's royal crown."[28]

The fort was finished, and the army divided, about a third being left as a garrison at Veracruz. The rest–between three and four hundred soldiers, and the few cavalry–were made ready for the march inland. Naturally he designated for service with him his most reliable men. But he was determined also to maintain a base on the coast. His ten remaining ships (one had been sent to Spain carrying the letters to King Charles) would be a standing invitation and temptation to the garrison to desert, and to the invasion force to retreat. In and act of astounding boldness which has ever since been associated with his name, Cortes scuttled nine of his ships, and came before his men to say:

> We already understand the expedition we are to make, and with
> the help of Our Lord Jesus Christ we must win all of our battles
> and encounters. If we are ever defeated, which God forbid, we
> can never raise our heads again, for there are so few of us, and
> we can expect no other help but His. Now that we no longer have
> ships in which to return to Cuba, we must depend upon our stout
> hearts and strong blows.[29]

As for the fainthearted, there was the one ship left; they could go back to Cuba in that. Naturally no one wanted to select himself for such a group, so Cortes scuttled the last ship as well.

Hernan Cortes and his three hundred Spaniards turned their backs to the shores of nightmare and their faces to the keep of the Hummingbird Wizard. If one estimates twenty per cent of the fifteen million people of the Aztec empire as men capable of bearing arms, the odds against them were precisely ten thousand to one.

Bernal Diaz, who was there, put it best:

> Let the curious reader see whether there is not much to ponder over
> in this which I venture to write, and whether there were ever in the
> universe men who had such daring.[30]

3.
The March and the Skulls (1519)

The Christian army departed from the town of Cempoal in Mexico on August 16, 1519. For three days they marched through coastal lowlands, then up the foothills and the higher slopes to Jalapa at 4,700-foot elevation, about fifty miles inland from Veracruz. They were still in the country of the friendly Totonacs, who provided guides and porters to carry their cannon, ammunition and essential baggage. "For ourselves, the poor soldiers," says Bernal Diaz, "we had need of no one, as we had nothing to carry but our arms, lances, muskets, crossbows, shields, and so on, with which we slept and marched. For shoes we had only *alpargatas* [cloth sandals with hemp soles]; but we were always ready for a fight."[31]

Upward they climbed beyond Jalapa, past a fortess-town built into the side of a mountain, out of Totonac country now, but no man's hand was raised against them. Montezuma, tortured by indecision, doubt and dark forebodings, had given orders for the time being not to oppose them openly, and even to supply them with some provisions for their journey. They crossed a high divide by a jagged, formidable pass, which Cortes said was rougher and steeper than any in Spain; they called it Nombre de Dios, Name of God. On its western slopes were villages and another Aztec fortress. Beyond that was a bleak, barren, windswept 7,000-foot plateau, a basin ringed by dead volcanoes extending round from towering Star Mountain, Orizaba. All the water was salt; there was no food. A hailstorm swept the waste, the ice bullets bouncing and clanging off the mail of the soldiers, which was all they had to wear for warmth. Two nights they camped in this forbidding wilderness. On the third day they mounted to another pass, where they found a small temple surrounded by stacks of firewood. Then they descended steeply, marching in close order on constant alert, to a place called Zocotlan (today Zautla), which reminded some of the soldiers of their villages at home. Something about it particularly suggested a Portuguese village called Castilblanco, to the Portuguese soldiers in the army who knew that town.

But Zocotlan of the Aztec empire was really not in the least like Castilblanco of the Christian kingdom of Portugal.

Its chief, Olintetl, sacrificed no less than fifty men just before the Spaniards arrived, on Montezuma's orders, and made a great effort to impress the Spaniards with Montezuma's wealth and power and the impregnability of Mexico City, of which Cortes now heard the first full description, with emphasis on its location on the water and how easy this made its defense.

Bernal Diaz and his fellows refused to be impressed. "The more he told us about the great fortresses and the bridges," he says, "the more we wanted to try our luck against them."[32]

Cortes gave a formal reply, through Aguilar and the dauntless Marina as always:

> I would have you know that we have come from afar at the order of our lord and king, the emperor Don Carlos, who has many great lords as his vassals. He sends a command to your great Montezuma that he is not to sacrifice or kill any more Indians, or rob his vassals, or take lands, but is to obey our lord and king. And to you, Olintetl, and to all the chiefs with you, I say the same. Give up your sodomy and all your other evil practices, for so commands Our Lord God, Whom we believe and whom we adore, Who gives us life and death and will raise us to heaven.[33]

The chiefs of Zocotlan listened sullenly, without replying. Cortes proposed erecting a cross, as he had done elsewhere. This time Father Olmedo vetoed it: "I do not think the time has come to leave a cross in the charge of these people, because they are without shame and without fear. As they are vassals of Montezuma, they may burn it or do something else that is evil."[34]

Before night fell, Bernal Diaz went to Zocotlan's central plaza. By the temple were enormous racks of skulls, with regular rows making it easy to count them by multiplication. Each skull represented a victim of sacrifice. Their number, he said, "might be one hundred thousand, and I say again, *one hundred thousand*."[35]

In the army of Cortes was a fellow townsman of Bernal Diaz named Francisco de Lugo, a brave officer, the illegitimate son of a wealthy merchant, in the New World to make the fortune which the accident of his birth had so far denied him. He was a long way from the golden fields and rich fairs of Medina del Campo now. His big greyhound, one of the dogs accompanying the expedition whose aspect seemed so fearful to the Mexicans, barked and howled all through that night in Zocotlan–probably sensing danger, perhaps even helping by his alertness to prevent it from materializing. But Francisco de Lugo's big greyhound may only have been baying at moonlight filtered through the jaws and eye sockets of one hundred thousand human skulls.

When the sun had come up next morning out of the eastern sea the Spaniards had left behind them, the almost infinitely long road home, Cortes went to Olintetl to ask him about the best road to Mexico City.

Olintetl recommended that they go by way of the city of Cholula; but the Cempoalans recommended that he go via Tlaxcala instead. Tlaxcala was a small republic entirely surrounded by Aztec territory, which had preserved its independence by constant warfare. Tlacaelle had never moved against Tlaxcala in full force because the almost constant Aztec wars with Tlaxcala provided a steady flow of prisoners for sacrifice. There are dark hints in the Mexican native histories of collusion between some Tlaxcalan leaders and Montezuma, before the Spaniards came, to keep up the warfare and make sure neither side won, that Tlaxcalan chiefs were even present in disguise in the rose-covered boxes by the temple of Huitzilopochtli watching their compatriots sacrificed. The story is told of Tlaxcala's greatest commander, Tlalhuicole, who was captured by the Aztecs, that refusing either to enter Montezuma's service or to accept freedom from him, he demanded the death in gladiatorial battle which was sometimes employed instead of sacrifice for the bravest warriors, and killed eight full-armed Aztec soldiers with nothing but a club before he fell–probably knowing his traitorous chiefs were watching, knowing no other way to demonstrate once and for all his detestation of everything the Aztec empire and its collaborators stood for. Men of Tlalhuicole's mettle, with a century of warfare behind them and no future (until now) but more of the same, would be the best allies Cortes could find.

But if the Tlaxcalans could hardly even trust their own leaders, they were still less inclined to trust the Cempoalan ambassadors whom Cortes sent to them. The ambassadors were heard politely, but were not permitted to return to Cortes. He waited fruitlessly in the little town of Ixtacamaxtitlan (where he felt as least safer then in Zocotlan with its hundred thousand skulls) until the last day of August, when he decided to press on regardless. Riding with six horsemen well in advance of his army, Cortes was the first to see a looming stone wall blocking the valley which provided the only easy access to Tlaxcala–a wall solidly constructed, nine feet high and twenty feet thick. Though at the moment undefended, it was a daunting obstacle, quite obviously a trap which could close behind them. After a pause before it, Cortes picked up the standard with the motto of Constantine and repeated its words: "Let us follow our flag with the sign of the cross and we shall conquer."[36] His men responded that God was their strength. They passed through and open gate in the wall, and on into the territory of Tlaxcala.

Three days of battle followed. Three thousand Tlaxcalans fruitlessly attacked the Spaniards in the afternoon of August 31; six thousand attacked the next day, causing a prolonged struggle in which one of the precious Spanish horses, a mare ridden by Pedro de Moron, was killed by a single blow of an obsidian-bladed broadsword. On September 4 the Tlaxcalans brought up their entire army of fifty thousand men. The next day the Spaniards would have to give battle against odds of nearly two hundred to one. The two priests with the army spent all night hearing the confessions of men preparing for the likelihood of death on the morrow.

On September 5 every man who could stand was put into line. With the wall behind them and a foe like this before them, it was virtually certain that in case of defeat, there would be no survivors.

As it happened, not all the Tlaxcalans attacked with vigor. There was deep division in their councils on who the extraordinary strangers really were, what they really wanted, and how to deal with them. Some thought that, since they had arrived with the Cempoalans who have been under Montezuma's rule, they were secretly in league with Montezuma. Others thought they might really be gods, but wanted to test them first. And there was a substantial element, in the militaristic atmosphere and bitter isolation of Tlaxcala, who were simply resolved to fight any invader to the death. These attacked with all their might on September 5, and were at least half the Tlaxacalan host. The odds were therefore still a hundred to one.

Like all Mexican armies, the Tlaxcalans were trained to take prisoners for sacrifice rather than to kill on the battlefield. It was very difficult to capture Spanish soldiers (though the Mexicans did it on quite a number of occasions) because they supported and protected one another so well. The horses were a great aid, but there were only twelve of them left. In the melee of hand-to-hand fighting there were only a few good opportunities to use the cannon and the primitive muskets; the battle was far from decided by Spanish technological superiority, though that did help. When all reasons and explanation are given, the fact remains that just over three hundred Spanish soldiers defeated some thirty thousand of the finest warriors in Mexico almost entirely with swords and crossbows. By any standard it was an extraordinary feat of arms.

Cortes and Bernal Diaz both explicitly attributed the victory to the direct intervention of God. When Montezuma heard the astonishing news, he was all the more sure that the invaders were gods.

Nearly every man in the army was wounded. It was a night of pain. The forty-five dead were buried deep so that the Indians would not find them and use their bodies in their ghastly rituals. There was no oil or salt for treating the wounds; there were no warm clothes or blankets. A cold wind moaned down from the nearby mountains. "Our lances, muskets and crossbows made a poor covering," says Bernal Diaz in his best laconic style, "although we slept more peacefully than we had done the night before."[37]

But even yet the Tlaxcalans were not ready to make peace. They did not attack again in great force but kept probing. They tried a night attack after their magicians told them that the strangers' strength left them when the sun set. The Spaniards were exhausted, cold, and crippled. Cortes was sick with fever. As he wrote frankly to King Charles:

> I assure Your Majesty that there was amongst us not one who was not very much afraid, seeing how deep into this country we were and among so many hostile people and so entirely without hope of help from anywhere.[38]

They took counsel with one another, and with the Indian girl Marina, who never showed a sign of weakness and never left Cortes' side except for combat itself. It was for this reason that the Indians named Cortes Malinche, "the captain of Marina." In camp there were murmurings against Cortes, finally surfacing in a formal proposal to return to the coast, build a ship and send for aid. Cortes replied by a ringing appeal to the Spanish crusading spirit:

> The greater the king we seek, the wider the land, the more numerous the enemy, so much the greater will be our glory, for have you not heard it said, *the more Moors, the greater the spoils?* Besides, we are obligated to exalt and increase our Holy Catholic Faith, which we undertook to do like good Christians, uprooting idolatry, that great blasphemy to our God, abolishing sacrifices and the eating of human flesh, which is so contrary to nature and so common here.[39]

> Isn't it true, gentlemen, that when we consider well all we have accomplished, surely it must be because God is helping us? Because He has preserved us from such great danger, let us hope that He will continue to do so.[40]

In the end, Christian courage and faith prevailed. The Tlaxcalans opened peace negotiations, while new ambassadors from Montezuma arrived offering Cortes virtually any amount of treasure if he would stay out of Mexico City (now only sixty miles away) and warning him on no account to trust the Tlaxcalans or ally himself with them. Cortes kept the Mexican ambassadors in his camp, by not returning them a definite answer, until he had a last made peace with Tlaxcala despite them. He waited to do this until all four of the principal chieftains of Tlaxcala came to him in a body to make a personal appeal that he enter their city and accept their friendship and alliance. Cortes agreed, and the alliance was concluded. He now had on his side a martial republic consisting of 150,000 families, which had tried his resolution and knew his quality, and hated the Aztec empire with all the accumulated hatreds of a hundred years of constant warfare and suspected treachery. The adherence of Tlaxcala was to save his life, his mission, and his conquest. Within a few years Tlaxcala was to produce the first Mexican Christian martyr, to be so thoroughly converted that it was sending out missionaries of its own to the rest of Mexico.

But that time was not yet. Cortes' first attempts to explain the Faith to the Tlaxcalans immediately were hardly comprehended. He could not even persuade them altogether to give up human sacrifice. The best he could do was to transform one of their temples into a church, where Mass was said and some baptisms administered. Shortly before, Cortes had written to Juan de Escalante, his commander at Veracruz, ordering up the extra altar wine and hosts for the Mass which he had carefully set aside, since the supply for the army on the march was nearly exhausted. It was the first communication Cortes had sent to the coast since the march began. Hernan Cortes had no intention of pushing on into the domain of the Hummingbird Wizard without the Body and Blood of Christ.

The Spaniards had entered Tlaxcala September 23, and there Cortes gave them a much needed three weeks' rest. But not all rested. Fascinated by the periodic small eruptions of towering Popocatapetl frowning over Tlaxcala directly to the west, between it and Mexico City, Diego de Ordaz asked permission to climb it. Ordaz was a captain of infantry and knight of Santiago, "very valiant, wise, strong, and of good nature, of a masculine countenance, and a black thin beard."[41] Cortes turned his request into an order, and Ordaz climbed the volcano, 18,000 feet high, which for an hour during their ascent threw out tongues of flame, plumes of ashes, and red hot stones. The awed Indians remained behind in their temples on the slope; Ordaz and his two Spanish companions defied the gods. Near Popocatapetl's boiling crater they found sulfur deposits usable for making gunpowder. On the way up they saw a good road over the shoulder of the volcano leading toward the Aztec capital, and followed it for enough to be able to look out over the whole splendid panorama of the valley of Anahuac with its lakes, centered by Mexico City, their objective.

Though there were still a few among the Spaniards, and more among the Indian allies, who counselled against going on to Mexico City itself, few could have any real doubt now that Cortes would never stop short of it. Furthermore, Cortes received from the Tlaxcalans his first connected and reasonably detailed account of the Quetzalcoatl legend, which explained much that had been mysterious to him in the behavior of Montezuma and his emissaries. Quite possibly this revelation was a major influence on his decision regarding his next route of march. The Tlaxcalans wanted him to go through Guaxocingo, a city allied with them and on the most direct route to Mexico City, but Montezuma's latest ambassadors, whom he still had with him, were insistent in urging that he go to the semi-independent city of Cholula to the southwest, which contained the most famous temple dedicated to Quetzalcoatl in all Mexico. The Tlaxcalans warned him that he was being lured into an ambush. Nevertheless it was to Cholula that Cortes went, quite likely concluding that he stood only to gain from any further association with a center of the worship of Quetzalcoatl, whatever might happen there. In that expectation, as so often, he was right.

Though still sometimes disputed, the evidence is very strong that there was a major Aztec plot to destroy Cortes and his army at Cholula. By now the Spaniards had been in the land long enough, and had become well enough known, so that the majority of Montezuma's councillors no longer believed they were really gods or emissaries of Quetzalcoatl. Montezuma still seemed to believe it, but his chief gods were enemies of Quetzalcoatl, and in his confusion and despair he began to think that it was now the will of Tezcatlipoca and Huitzilopochtli that Cortes and his men be killed. And if his councilors were right and Cortes was not Quetzalcoatl or his representative, then there could be no better place than Cholula to destroy him; for Cholula was Quetzalcoatl's holy city and its priests had long insisted that any unbelieving and sacrilegious army penetrating its precincts would be drowned by torrents of water issuing from its great temple pyramind.

This threat and claim of the god's special guardianship of Cholula were implicitly believed in Mexico. They accounted for Cholula's semi-independent political status. It was even believed that any gap which opened in the masonry of the temple pyramid created a danger of accidentally unleashing the deluge, with the result that every crack was sealed as soon as it was discovered by a special cement made from lime and the blood of sacrificed children from two to three years old.

Cortes marched to Cholula in the middle of October 1519. At the strongly worded request of its leaders, he asked his Tlaxcalan allies to remain outside the town, in view of the long history of hostility between Tlaxcala and Cholula. He and his men then entered the city, watched by an immense throng, with Father Olmedo beside Cortes carrying a crucifix. The people and their leaders were curious but cold. Their supplies to their guests were niggardly. Some streets were walled off and holes dug in them. New messengers from Montezuma arrived, but did not come to Cortes. On the second night the Spaniards were in Cholula there was a special secret sacrifice of seven people–five of them children–to the god of war. And on the third night, before their planned departure the next morning, the wife of a Cholulan chief came to Marina to urge her to take refuge at the chief's house so that she would not be massacred with the Spaniards, for the chief's wife wanted Marina to marry her son. Marina pretended to go along with her plan, drew from her all the information she had about the plot, and then ran to tell Cortes. He arrested and confined the chief's wife, along with a Cholulan leader from whom he extracted a full confession.

The next morning some three thousand armed Cholulan warriors assembled, allegedly to accompany the Spaniards in their march to Mexico City. Cortes locked them in the central courtyard. Suddenly appearing there on horseback, with Marina as ever at his side, he taxed them with their intended treachery, contrasted it with the honorable open war the Tlaxcalans had at first waged against the Spaniards, and told them the gods to whom they were planning to sacrifice their Spanish victims had no power over Christians.

The chiefs replied admitting that they had planned to kill the Spaniards, but blaming Montezuma and his orders for everything. Cortes responded inexorably that they must die. He fired a signal gun and set upon them. It was no "massacre," as some have called it, but a battle, for the Cholulans were armed and murderous, and they fought for nearly five hours. But they were surrounded, and almost all of them were killed. The battle spread through the whole city, and the Tlaxcalans who had been camped outside arrived after two hours to join in it. The fighting engulfed the great temple of Quetzalcoatl. Its idol was hurled down and the building was fired, consuming many of the priests. On its high platform of death the victors erected a great cross–not of wood this time, but of stone.

The shock seemed to paralyze the whole Aztec empire. The news spread like wildfire through the entire Mexican culture area, even to Yucatan, that Quetzalcoatl had failed to defend himself, his most revered shrine, and his people. And the terrible invaders were still coming on. A message came to Montezuma from Cortes that he knew Aztecs had been involved in the plot at Cholula, that many had told him that it was done by Montezuma's orders, that it seemed to him now that the emperor "did not keep his word or speak the truth." Consequently, Cortes now "intended to enter his land at war doing all the harm he could as an enemy."[42] Montezuma collapsed; for eight days he betook himself in silent retreat to the House of the Serpent, while a parade of human sacrifices was ordered in the hope that somehow this would give him inspiration. He was presented with the head of a dead Spaniard, which he contemplated lugubriously for hours. So it was Montezuma's council, not the emperor himself, that had to make the decision finally to invite the Spaniards into the capital, since there was no other choice short of all-out war.

The Spaniards left Cholula on November 1st for the last stages of their magnificent march: first the scouts, then the cannon, then the horsemen, then the infantry. Bernal Diaz says, using a Spanish soldier's expressions: "I can see myself as we advanced, my beard always over my shoulder."[43] For the Aztecs, that column marching relentlessly onward, closer and closer, loomed gigantic and grotesque through a haze of fear and foreshadowing of judgment.

> When the massacre at Cholula was complete, the strangers set out again toward the City of Mexico. They came in battle array, as conquerors, and the dust rose in whirlwinds on the roads. Their spears glinted in the sun, and their pennons fluttered like bats. They made a loud clamor as they marched, for their coats of mail and their weapons clashed and rattled. Some of them were dressed in glistening iron from head to foot; they terrified everyone who saw them.
>
> Their dogs came with them, running ahead of the column. They raised their muzzles high, they lifted their muzzles to the wind. They raced on with saliva dripping from their jaws.[44]

Two days later, Montezuma said starkly:

> We will be judged and punished. And however it may be, and whenever it may be, we can do nothing but wait.[45]

That night the Spaniards camped at Calpan, whose people were allies of Tlaxcala, and therefore friendly. They told Cortes there were two roads he could take between the two mighty mountains, Popocatapetl (The Mountain That Smokes) and Iztaccihuatl (The White Women): the usual, open road to Chalco at the southeastern edge of the fifty-mile-long central lake of Mexico, and a road at a higher level that had been closed for lack of use. Cortes unhesitatingly chose the closed road. It led through a thick, gloomy pine forest past and over barricades of tree trunks. The soldiers toiled upward. From the top of the pass they could all see for the first time the rich, teeming Valley of Anahuac, heartland of the Mexican civilization.

> Suddenly, the plain with its two lakes, and its thirty cities, sprang into view in the bright sun, calling forth in their minds visions of the enchanted cities they had read or heard of in the books of chivalry....[Mexico City's] adobe houses were spotlessly white with plaster and shone like silver in the pure air of the high tableland, while its teocallis [temples] rose above them with the quiet majesty of their cubic lines. The chief impression was one of power and greatness, unlike anything that the Discovery had as

42

yet revealed. For the first time the dreams of Colon [Columbus] came true. The eager and hungry expressed their high hopes in typical Spanish language: "This is the promised land." To which in no less typical Spanish, others commented: "The more the Moors, the better the spoils." But the opposition grumbled and, awed by the immensity of what they saw, their hearts sank in dismay. "We are tempting God," they said, "if we let ourselves into that danger, so few in the midst of so many." Cortes noticed the state of mind of his men. Promises here and appeals to Spanish valor there, soon claimed the fears of the less brave, and the army marched on.[46]

As suddenly as the great view had been spread before them, dark gray clouds rolled in and it began to snow, caking on the ground. The army descended six miles to some mountain rest houses where they spent the night in front of roaring fires.

About this time Montezuma emerged from his fruitless retreat, having found no answers to his cosmic and personal questions. There were still counselors who urged him to military resistance against the strangers, but after Cholula he dared not try that. Nor could he deceive himself into believing that they really came in friendship. There remained only sorcery and magic. Montezuma sent a double of himself to Cortes to see what he would do with him (he was scornfully dismissed); he sent a large party of sorcerers, who returned stricken with fear, claiming to have seen an apparition of Tezcatlipoca as a drunken peasant, and of Mexico City in flames; other sinister figures prowled about Cortes' camp by night. Cortes had no idea who they were or what they were doing, but he didn't like the look of them; he ordered his sentinels to shoot any suspicious persons on sight after dark, and some of them were shot. So well was the order carried out that crossbowman Martin Lopez came within a second or two of killing Cortes himself on night rounds. Said the blunt-spoken Castilian to his commander: "Next time, sir, do speak from a longer distance."[47]

Down from the high slopes to the great lake they came, the standard of the Cross and the motto of Constantine flying in the van, then infantry, horseman, crossbowmen, horsemen again, and musketeers, their steps resolutely forward, still with "the beard over the shoulder," still against the odds of ten thousand to one. They had marched halfway across the realm of the Hummingbird Wizard, never losing a battle, and were about to enter his ultimate stronghold. "We marched by short journeys," says Bernal Diaz, "commending ourselves to God and His good mother, Our Lady, and talked about how we should enter the city, while our hearts filled with hope that, as Our Lord Jesus Christ had guarded us from danger in the past, He would also protect us from the power of Mexico."[48]

The Spaniards spent the night of Sunday, November 6, at Ayotzinco on the Lake of Mexico. Two days later, on Tuesday the 8th, they marched out upon the great eastern causeway leading to Mexico City in the middle of the lake. The causeway was wide enough for eight horsemen to have ridden abreast. Immense crowds had gathered; every tower and terrace was black with people, and the waters of the lake were covered with canoes. Where a second causeway joined that upon which the Spaniards marched, a thousand prominent citizens in brilliant array greeted the strangers. Here there was a strong fort; it was the entrance to Mexico City itself. Beyond the fort was a wooden bridge "ten paces wide" across a gap in the causeway, which allowed the waters of the lake to flow back and forth, and could be removed as needed for the defense of the city. Beyond the bridge was a long, wide, straight and beautiful avenue, lined with houses and temples. Along it, to meet Cortes, came Montezuma. Cortes dismounted from his horse to greet him.

Christ, who died to save all men and holds all power in Heaven and on Earth, had come, now in the person of His champions, to claim His own in a land that had never known Him and had been dedicated to the service of His ancient enemy. Christ's conquest of Mexico would not be achieved by swords and crossbows, political craft and diplomacy, nor even by the magnificent valor of the soldiers of Catholic Spain, for His kingdom is not of this world. But these men, by these means, would prepare and open up His way, make His paths straight through what had been a wilderness of horror and hellish sin, transforming Mexico into a place which His mother could visit.

In the eloquent words of Salvador de Madariaga:

> Thus on that fateful Tuesday, November 8th, 1519, third day of Quecholli, 8th Ehecatl of the year 1-Reed of the eighth sheaf, the two men stood before each other, looking into each others' eyes. But the eyes of the Mexican were closed lakes, soon to dry up under the sun of another knowledge; while in the eyes of Cortes there lived the endless sea.[49]

4.

In the Keep
of the Hummingbird Wizard
(1519-1520)

The fantastic three months that followed the first entry of Cortes into Mexico City provide one of the great climaxes of history, rivalling the taking of Jerusalem by the First Crusade, the reconquest of Seville by King St. Ferdinand, the massacres of September and the Thermidorian reaction in the French Revolution, the Battle of Waterloo, and the Red October of 1917 in Russia. Yet this one is unique, different from all the others, in the incredible speed with which it had developed. The other climaxes marked culminations of chains of events going back for years or centuries. But Cortes and his army had been in Mexico less than seven months. On November 8, 1519 Cortes entered its capital as the honored guest of the absolute ruler of fifteen million people, as one who might be a god, or at least the emissary of a god; by November 14 Montezuma was Cortes' prisoner, and Cortes was–however precariously–ruling Mexico through him. Yet Cortes, too, was a prisoner of the Hummingbird Wizard, because he was unable to free the beautiful city from its hideous grip without provoking an uprising that would cost him his conquest.

The first week, which sets the stage, divides itself into two parts: from Tuesday to Saturday in the week of their arrival; and from Sunday to Tuesday of the following week.

When the two men met, Montezuma greeted Cortes as though he were indeed Quetzalcoatl himself.

> Now you have arrived on the earth. You have come to your city, Mexico. You have come here to sit on your throne, to sit under its canopy. . . . No, it is not a dream. I am not walking in my sleep. I am not seeing you in my dreams . . . I have seen you at last! I was in agony for five days, for ten days, with my eyes fixed on the Region of the Mystery. And now you have come out of the clouds and mists to sit on your throne again.
> This was foretold by the kings who governed your city, and now it has taken place. You have come back to us; you have come down from the sky. Rest now, and take possession of your royal house. Welcome to your land, my lords![50]

Cortes replied graciously, and Montezuma, after adorning him with two precious necklaces and giving many other tokens of honor, led them to the great palace of his father, Emperor Axayacatl. So large was this building that it easily accommodated all the Spaniards, the 2,000 Tlaxcalan auxiliaries, and the numerous servants Montezuma designated to wait on them. Montezuma offered Cortes a throne wrought in gold and studded with precious stones, and invited him to partake of a sumptuous repast.

Cortes thanked him; but before dining, he carefully emplaced his cannon and stationed his sentries.

After dinner Montezuma came for an evening visit. To Bernal Diaz he seemed about forty, though he was actually fifty-two, slender and moderately tall, with light brown skin, grave, very clean in his person. He did not look or act like a monster. Many of the Spaniards later came to like him personally. He spoke again of Cortes as the man whose coming had been foretold by the ancient prophecies. Cortes, replying, made no claim to be Quetzalcoatl. (He was both too faithful a Catholic and too wise a man to make any such claim, though a lesser man would have been tempted to try it under the apparently favorable circumstances.) Instead he spoke of King Charles, his master, to whom Montezuma ought to give allegiance as well. Montezuma, in all probability seeing Charles as a god, perhaps even the High God Ometecuhtli as mentioned earlier, said that he would do so. On that encouraging note the two men parted, and the Spaniards spent a quiet night.

Dawn came up like thunder. Directly opposite the palace of Axayacatl where the Spaniards were staying was the great temple of the Hummingbird Wizard, the very temple that Tlacaellel had dedicated thirty-two years before by cutting out the hearts of eighty thousand men. At first light the daily sacrifices began: cool quails, black and white birds symbolizing the death of the starry night just past, and men, whom Huitzilopochtli always wanted. The Spaniards in the palace could actually see the blood running down the steps of the temple pyramid–and most of it did not come from quails. On the other side of the palace of Axayacatl from the temple was the zoo. Its carnivores were fed daily on the trunks of the bodies of the sacrificed men. The beasts saw and heard and smelt their breakfast. A cacophony of hideous noise broke out. "I might as well tell all the infernal things now," says Bernal Diaz, visibly screwing up his courage–and few men ever had more– "when the tigers and lions [jaguars and pumas] roared, and the jackals [coyotes] and foxes howled, and the snakes hissed, it was horrible to hear; it seemed like Hell."[51]

We have an almost hour-by-hour account from Bernal Diaz of these incredible days, but we long to know even more. Where was crossbowman Martin Lopez, whose answer to witches and warlocks and creatures of the night was his trusty iron-headed quarrel? Was he on watch that morning? Where was Francisco de Lugo's bog greyhound? Did he send back his deep bay in answer to the howls of the man-eaters? The temple was within easy cannon shot. Did any of the cannoneers propose opening fire?

Yet all around was a clear blue morning; the sun shone, the air was cool and bracing, the lake gleamed, the golden corn tassels waved in the breeze. God was still good, and He still ruled the cosmos. But His enemy ruled Cactus Rock–and the Christian army was inside.

Cortes rose. His was now a responsibility so great as hardly to bear thinking on. "Some things must be done rather than thought," he had once told Governor Velazquez of Cuba.[52] He resolved to go to see Montezuma at once, accompanied by four of his officers and five of his men. The officers were sunny, red-haired Alvarado; strong black-bearded Ordaz who had climbed erupting Popocatapetl; Juan Velazquez de Leon, with a curly red beard and a rough fierce voice, superlatively brave but hot-tempered, who had killed a man in Hispaniola and was to die at the bridge of death on the Night of Sorrow at the end of the coming June; and Gonzalo de Sandoval, "the constant captain,"[53] only twenty-two years old but rapidly developing into Cortes' most reliable subordinate, with curly light brown hair, "a plain man, not avaricious of gold,"[54] a native of Cortes' own Medellin, whose father had commanded a castle in the wars of the reconquest. One of the five common soldiers Cortes selected was Bernal Diaz. (In all probability Marina and Aguilar went too, as interpreters, though Bernal Diaz does not mention them.)

Montezuma welcomed them himself in his spacious palace, with a hundred rooms each with a bath; walls of marble, jasper, porphyry, and alabaster; ceilings of cedar, cypress, and palm-wood; floors covered with rich thick carpets. He took Cortes' hand and seated him on his right, and bade all the other Spaniards sit on chairs nearby, while he was joined by several of his nephews. Cortes declared that he would now explain in detail and in person to Montezuma what he had already often told him through ambassadors: that his essential reason for coming to Mexico was to bring him and his people the knowledge of the One True God Who created and rules the universe, and the good news of Christ who died to save all men and rose again; that all men, wherever they live in the world, are brothers who should worship the One True God together; that it is wrong to worship idols and sacrifice men to them; and that one of his principal purposes in coming was to stop the great evil of human sacrifice. As for himself and his men, they were only rough soldiers, no more than heralds of Christ; in times to come "our lord and king would send men who lead holy lives, better than ourselves, who would explain everything, for we had come only to notify them."[55]

47

"Here we have always worshiped our own gods and hold them to be good," Montezuma replied coldly. "So must yours be. For the present do not talk to us about them any more."[56]

Montezuma went on to assure Cortes that the bad reports he had heard about him from his Indian enemies, especially the Tlaxcalans, were false. Cortes responded that he should not concern himself with such stories, but instead make friends with Tlaxcala in particular, for the sake of peace. Montezuma was unenthusiastic about that idea, but sent the Spaniards away with some more presents.

During the next several days it appears that Montezuma held a series of meetings with his advisors to discuss what action might or should be taken with regard to the Spaniards, and who they really were; but as before, no conclusion or firm decision was reached. Meanwhile, the Spaniards slept in their clothes, their weapons by their side. All the rest of his life Bernal Diaz kept the night habits he had acquired during his weeks in the keep of the Hummingbird Wizard, sleeping in his clothes, without a bed. But he would get up from time to time, "to look at the sky and stars and walk a little in the night dew,"[57] reassuring himself that he was, thanks be to God, a free man under the open sky, that he really had escaped the obsidian knife of Witchywolves that had claimed the lives of so many of his fellows.

On Sunday, November 13, the Lord's day, Cortes told Montezuma that it was his wish to visit the principal marketplace of the city and the great temple with most of his men. All the Spaniards were much impressed by the opulence of the market, which was some distance from the temple located near the palace.[58] Montezuma went directly there, to sacrifice some boys before the Spaniards arrived. When they came to the plaza facing the temple, they marvelled at its size–bigger than the famous plaza of Salamanca in Spain–and the cleanliness and brilliance of its white stone paving. But their eyes were soon drawn to a building about a stone's throw from the main gate of the temple. It was in the form of a theater, with towers at both ends, and more than seventy tall poles studded from top to bottom with spikes. The towers were constructed solely of human skulls and mortar. The walls, steps and benches were constructed of stones and human skulls. Each spike on the poles bore five skulls impaled through the temples. Andres de Tapia and Gonzalo de Umbria counted 136,000 skulls exclusive of those in the towers, which being constructed entirely of skulls, probably had at least that many more.[59]

The Spaniards climbed with some difficulty the 114 steps to the top of the temple pyramid. Montezuma sent priests to help Cortes up, but he would not let them touch him. From the top was a splendid view of the entire city, the lake, and the satellite cities on its shores. Confident that there were no Indians at hand who understood Spanish, Cortes said to his men: "Truly, my heart tells me that from here many kingdoms and dominions will be conquered, for here is the capital wherein the devil had his main seat; once this city has been subdued and mastered, the rest will be easy to conquer."[60]

Atop the pyramid was a chapel which contained the images of the two great gods to which the sacrifices were made: Huitzilopochtli and Tezcatlipoca. Cortes, after being told by Father Olmedo that it was not at all a good idea then to try to build a church on the temple platform, asked Montezuma to let him see the gods. After a brief consultation, Montezuma agreed to let all the Spaniards see them, though the sight of these images was normally restricted to the priests and the highest nobility. A heavy curtain was drawn aside. The scene within was driven into Bernal Diaz's memory as though by a red-hot iron, not a whit less vivid after the passage of fifty years, when this untutored soldier wrote a description of it whose nightmarish horror might have come from the pen of Edgar Allan Poe– but this scene was not fiction; it was *real*.

> On each altar there were two statues, as of giants, and very fat, and the first, on the right side, they say was that of Witchywolves, their god of war, and his face and front were very wide, and his eyes out of shape and horrible, and so many rich stones and gold pearls and pearl seed stuck to his body with sticking paste that all his body and head were covered with it; and girded to his body some kind of big snakes, made of gold and rich stones; and in one hand a bow, and arrows in the other. And another small idol close to him, who, they said, was his page, was holding a short spear for him, and a round buckler very rich of gold and stones; and, round his neck, the said Witchywolves was wearing some Indian faces and some hearts of Indians, some of gold, some of silver, with many blue stones, and there were many braziers with their incense, which is copal, and with the hearts of three Indians which they had sacrificed that day and were burning, and the walls of that chapel were so steeped black with crusts of blood, and the floor also, that it stank very badly. . . . The other big image, as tall as Witchywolves, had a face like a bear, and eyes that shone, made of their mirrors, which they call *tezcat*, and the body stuck all over with rich stones, just like that of Witchywolves, for, they said, the two were brothers and this Tezcatlipoca was the god of hell and he was in charge of the souls of the Mexicans; and close to his body he had some figures like small devils with tails like serpents, and on the walls so much blood, and the floor soaked in it, that in the slaughterhouses of Castile the stench was not worse.[61]

All the more, now, did Hernan Cortes know exactly where he was–
and what needed to be done about it. He turned to the emperor
Montezuma. White teeth under his long black mustache flashed in a
steely, mirthless smile.

> I cannot understand how so great a lord and wise a man as you
> are has not yet thought it out that these idols are not gods, but
> very bad things known as devils; and so that you may come to
> know them as such, and all your priests see it clearly, grant me as
> a favor that we set up a Cross on top of this tower, and we shall
> set aside one part of these chapels, where Witchywolves and
> Tezcatlipoca now are, for an image of Our Lady, and you shall
> see what fear these idols will then feel.[62]

The priests glowered, and Montezuma declared that Cortes had
insulted his gods. The Spaniards climbed down the 114 steep steps. At
the bottom, "they were shown the room where the dead bodies of victims,
rolled down the pyramid after the hearts had been cut out, were collected
and cut up, and where the limbs reserved for the priests were cooked."[63]

Cortes had one more request to make of Montezuma that day. He
asked permission to build a chapel in the palace where they were staying.
Permission was given. The chapel was built in two days, with a cross set
up and an image of the Blessed Virgin Mary. Mass was said there every
day, and every day Bernal Diaz and many of the other soldiers knelt there
to sing the Ave Maria.

During the construction of the chapel, a discovery was made which
was ultimately to reveal all too clearly that this Christian army, despite
its glorious heroism and its God-given mission, was composed after all of
sinners–and some great sinners. A hidden room was found with a treasure
accumulated and secreted by Montezuma's father the emperor Axayacatl,
builder of the palace where the Spaniards were staying. Cortes ordered
the hidden room sealed up again; not one precious object in it was taken.
But the men did not forget it was there; and in time it began to prey on
their minds. It has been said that Spanish conquistadores sought glory,
God, and gold, and indeed, almost all of them did seek all three. The
great question for each conquistador was the order of priority in which he
placed them. In every Spanish army there were men who truly put gold
first, who would sell their honor and even their souls for gold. At the
bridge of death on the Night of Sorrow, the cold mud bottom of salt lake
Texcoco was to be covered with the bodies of Spanish soldiers who had
been too weighted down with gold to be able effectively to march, fight,
flee, or swim.

But for the moment, everyone realized it was no time to be gold-hunting. The life of every man was at stake. Montezuma had not, despite his humble and submissive words at his first meeting with Cortes, really been prepared to turn his empire over to them. He had drawn the line at precisely the most important point: the continued rule of the devil-gods over Mexico City. Upon that, clearly, he was prepared to insist. So long as that continued, the Spaniards would be in constant and deadly danger.

Hernan Cortes never waited to be attacked. No commander has ever better appreciated the value of a bold offense. He never let himself be struck first. Surrounded by enemies natural and supernatural, he delivered suddenly, totally unexpectedly, a rapier-thrust into the vitals of the foe.

He took Emperor Montezuma prisoner on Tuesday, the 15th of November.

He had more than enough cause to do so. All his dealings with Montezuma, from his arrival in Mexico, had showed that the Aztec emperor wanted to stop the Spaniards or kill them, and had been restrained from effective action to this end only by his overactive imagination, his fears, and his guilt. These operated most strongly when their object was at a distance. Living literally next door to the Spaniards, he could hardly continue for very long to think of them as real gods. The more he learned, the more he was likely to suspect that even their sovereign overseas was no more than an earthly monarch like himself. Standing at the pinnacle of perhaps the most cruel system of oppressive rule that man and devil together have ever devised, short of a miracle of grace he was most unlikely to give it up. In their unique position in the heart of the enemy's capital, the Spaniards were protected only by the aura of strangeness and invincibility, which would soon begin to fade. Eventually–and probably sooner rather than later–they would simply be set upon and killed. Their chief weapons, cannon and cavalry, were not much use in a city built mostly on or over water; and they had no boats. Cortes must rule or die. Only through a captive Montezuma might he now realistically hope to rule, at least for a time, taking advantage of all the ingrained habits of obedience in a fully developed totalitarian public order.

Cortes made up his mind to act when, on the morning of the 15th, two of his Tlaxcalan allies brought him news of a clash near the coast between a Mexican force under a chief named Quauhpopoca and a detachment of the Spanish garrison at Veracruz, at which Juan de Escalante, the garrison commander, was killed. It appears–to the extent that conflicting reports on the episode can be disentangled and harmonized–that Quauhpopoca was acting under old orders from Montezuma to try to regain control of the coast for the Aztecs once Cortes had left it. But it was at least confirming evidence that Montezuma had always intended to hurt the Spaniards if and where he could. The story that this attack and that of Cholula were without Montezuma's knowledge and consent was absurd in such an absolute autocracy as the Aztec empire. Final and conclusive proof was provided by the fact that the head of a Spaniard killed in the skirmish with Escalante was sent directly to Montezuma. Cortes and thirty Spaniards went to Montezuma's rooms, taxed him with the Cholulan conspiracy and the latest incident with Quauhpopoca, arrested him, and ordered him to come with them to the palace of Axayacatl, where Cortes promised to honor him and maintain him in the style to which he was accustomed, but without letting him go. Montezuma naturally demurred. There were no less than four hours of argument. Finally the hot-tempered Juan Velazquez de Leon cried out that Montezuma should come with them at once or be killed. Montezuma asked Marina what he had said.

The Aztec girl, whose ancestors for generations had been taught to bow their heads so as never to look directly at the emperor, who had been cast out of his society like refuse, now standing tall and straight before him, caught and held his haunted black eyes with hers now fiercely bright. Her Nahauatl words were edged with ice.

> Lord Montezuma, my advice is to go with them to their quarters
> without any trouble. I know they will honor you as the great lord
> you are. Otherwise, you will be left dead.[64]

He came. He had already ordered Quauhpopoca and fifteen of his associates brought to Mexico City for judgment; when they arrived he turned them all over to Cortes, who condemned them to death, while taking their confessions which stated that they had acted on Montezuma's orders. Cortes ordered the sixteen men burned to death, chaining Montezuma briefly so that he had to watch it.

It has been argued that only such a death could have impressed people who inflicted death so frequently and bloodily as the Mexicans; and it certainly did impress them. The Mexicans were horrified by this painful and slow method of execution, and those who saw it or heard of it in detail were probably deterred from making any more attacks on Spaniards for a time. But, like all the burnings at the stake which were the ultimate penalty of that age in Christian Europe, it cannot really be defended. It was a touch of the kingdom of the dark angel behind the Hummingbird Wizard upon the kingdom of Christ.

Soon after the execution of Quauhpopoca, some time in December, Cortes decided to attempt to formalize and consolidate his position of effective control over the Aztec empire through Montezuma as his captive, by having Montezuma and his chief nobles swear allegiance to King Charles and deliver a substantial tribute in gold, silver and jewelry. Montezuma agreed, and many–though not all–of his great nobles followed suit. Montezuma actually wept as he explained that he was turning over his kingdom to the men of the prophecy, and as a seal of his sincerity, he presented them with the treasure of his father Axaycatl which they had discovered, earlier, but had forborne to touch.

The royal fifth of this fabulous treasure was quickly and honestly counted and faithfully set aside, though there was much unpleasant quarrelling among the Spaniards over the distribution of the remainder. It was about this time that Charles, far away in Spain, received his first communication from Cortes through his emissary Puertocarrero via the ship Cortes had sent to Spain in July. Charles was impressed, as he was still more impressed when some Mexican treasure arrived, at a critical moment in his career, as he held court at Valladolid in the Easter season of 1520, shortly before departing from Spain for several years to take up his duties as Holy Roman Emperor in Germany.

But Cortes and his men already knew that their unwilling hosts gave up gold and silver and jewels much more easily than they would give up their terrible gods. On December 12, with Cortes' permission, Montezuma had attended the great annual ceremonies at the central temple in honor of Tlaloc the rain god. Cortes ordered him to make no human sacrifices, and sent with him Father Olmedo along with sunny Alvarado; angry Velazquez de Leon; Francisco de Lugo the master of the greyhound; proud, impatient Alonso de Avila; and about half his army. They climbed the steep steps of the great temple pyramid and gazed upon the chapel on the top platform where the monsters hid. Several men and boys were sacrificed, Cortes' orders and Father Olmedo's protests notwithstanding. "As we couldn't do anything about it *then*," says Bernal Diaz, "we pretended not to notice."[65]

Cortes' hard logical mind, schooled by his recent astonishing experiences to take in and evaluate all sides of a profoundly alien situation, would have grasped quite soon the new and more subtle kind of mortal danger that now threatened him. If Montezuma had been the Devil's viceroy in Mexico, he, Hernan Cortes, was moving toward becoming the same. Montezuma had declared again and again that he had accepted captivity only because he was sure it was the will of Huitzilopochtli. *What if it was*? The Hummingbird Wizard might prefer to have Cortes. He would gladly let him have all the gold and precious stones in Mexico if Cortes would let some excuse be found for Huitzilopochtli's rule and the slaughter in the temples to continue, essentially unchanged. So far he had been unable to stop it. How soon might he become, insensibly, an accessory?

From thought Cortes sprang to action. He went to Montezuma with seven of his officers and a strong guard, and said to him:

> I have often asked you not to sacrifice any more souls to your gods, who are deceiving you, but you have not been willing to do so. We have come to beg you to give us leave to remove them and put up Our Lady, Santa Maria, and a cross. If you do not give permission, they [indicating his men] will do so anyway, and I would not like them to kill any priests.[66]

There is every reason to believe that Cortes was telling Montezuma no more than the simple truth about what his men, who had been watching and hearing the human sacrifices in the temple next to their quarters for two full months, were threatening to do.

Montezuma said he would see about it, while warning that any removal of the gods would lead to all-out war. He secured permission for the erection of an altar, a cross, and an image of the Blessed Virgin Mary in a room within the temple itself. It was cleaned and washed with lime; Father Olmedo said Mass there every day; an "older soldier" was stationed to guard the room (Can it have been only one? What a duty!), and the Aztec priests were ordered to keep the room clean and candles burning before the Cross and the image of Our Lady, and to decorate it with branches and flowers, but without touching the altar.

Who but Hernan Cortes ever arranged it so that the acolytes of Satan would have to burn candles to the Blessed Virgin Mary, on the orders of their earthly sovereign? The Devil hates above all to be laughed at, and there has rarely been a better laugh at his expense. Perhaps we may even dare to imagine a smile on the lips of Mary herself.

It was more than the Hummingbird Wizard could stand. The priests came to Montezuma and told him the Huitzilopochtli had spoken, and in no uncertain terms. Our Lady, the Cross, the altar, and the daily Mass must go from his temple at once, or there would be war.

Cortes replied that the Christian knights of Spain would gladly fight for the Lord God and for the Mother of God. He called his men to arms, and they marched straight on the temple with drawn swords. Up the tall steps of death they climbed to the platform at the top. With a slash of keen blades they ripped through the veil that hid the monsters from profane view.

"Oh God!" cried Cortes, "Why dost thou permit the devil to be so grossly honored in this land?"[67] He bowed his head, and added, as though in prayer: "Accept, O Lord, that we may serve Thee in this land."[68]

The chief priests came running and panting to the scene. Cortes told them he had come to cleanse and purge their shrine to evil, and place there the image of the Mother of God. The priests told him that the people were already taking arms against the Spaniards for what they were doing. Cortes sent a messenger to warn the rest of his men, and ordered up forty reinforcements. Then he turned and faced the Hummingbird Wizard. Its obscene bulk rose up before him as though to fill the earth and all the sky.

Somewhere near the door was a metal bar. Cortes seized it. He swung it over his head. "I pledge my faith as a gentleman, and swear to God that it is true," wrote Andres de Tapia, a valiant young officer of pale complexion and grave countenance, who has left us the best record of this supreme moment, "that I can see now how the Marquess [Cortes] leapt up in a supernatural way and swung forward holding the bar midway till he struck the idol high up on its eyes, and broke off its gold mask, saying: 'We must risk something for God'."[69]

A few days later the priests removed the idols from the great temple, in deathly silence. True to his word, Cortes ordered their shrines cleaned. In this process he discovered a hidden chamber with treasure–and the ashes of Tlacaellel. The Spaniards erected two altars and brought up images of the Blessed Virgin Mary and of St. Christopher. Heavily escorted by armed men, a cross, followed by the two images, was carried up the great staircase, scene of the unprecedented horror of Tlacaellel's sacrifice of the eighty thousand in 1487. The Spaniards sang *Te Deum laudamus*. Father Olmedo stepped forward.

> I will go up to the altar of God,
> The God who gives joy to my youth.

The soldiers of Christ took off their helmets. Holy Mass was said; Jesus Christ came, Body, Blood, Soul, and Divinity, to His altar now standing, like a meteor fallen from Heaven, in the very heart and center of what had been the keep of the Hummingbird Wizard.

5.
To The Night of Sorrow
(1520)

But the struggle was not over yet.

Within a very short time after the removal of the images of Huitzilopochtli and Tezcatlipoca from the great temple, Montezuma was observed deep in conversation with his priests, counselors and generals. The young Spanish page Orteguilla, who had picked up fluent Nahuatl and was constantly in attendance on the captive emperor, heard enough to warn Cortes that something very serious and dangerous was afoot.

Cortes went immediately to Montezuma, who said to him:

> How sorry I am about the answer we have had from our gods; it is that we are to make war on you and kill you and make you go away to the sea and beyond. . . . Before war begins, you had better leave this city and none of you remain here. Do this in any way convenient to you, for otherwise you will all be killed.[70]

Cortes responded that before he could leave Mexico he must have ships, since those he came in had all been sunk at Veracruz, and that Montezuma must come with him to visit King Charles. If the Spaniards were attacked while their ships were being built, they would fight with all their well-known prowess and valor, and great numbers of Mexicans would die.

Montezuma was most unhappy at the prospect of leaving Mexico City still a captive, but he agreed to order that no attack be made on the Spaniards so long as they were preparing to leave. He would propitiate Huitzilopochtli and Tezcatlipoca with sacrifices–but not with sacrifices of men. As Cortes wrote proudly to King Charles, he told Montezuma that human sacrifice was contrary to King Charles' laws, and "that he who kills shall be killed,"[71] and from that point on until the Spanish were forced out of the city, there were no more human sacrifices there. Even under constant threat of war and death for his own men, Cortes held the shield of the Christian army over the despised victims of the Aztec death factory. For three months the immemorial bloodshed ceased in Cactus Rock.

Some modern writers have unblushingly called it folly. Hernan Cortes would have called it keeping the Faith.

Lent came, and Holy week. Three Spanish ships were under construction at Veracruz. We cannot be sure what Cortes had in mind at this point. Bernal Diaz says the master shipwright later told him that he was hurrying to work to completion, believing this to be Cortes' genuine wish; for once the later account of Cortes' secretary in Spain, Francisco Lopez de Gomara, rings more true; he has Cortes instructing that the work of shipbuilding go as slowly as possible, in confidence that "God our Lord, on whose business we are, will provide men and help us to save this good country."[72]

More men came indeed, almost a thousand Spaniards in a dozen ships; but their mission was not to aid or save Cortes and his endangered heroes, but to destroy them. They arrived in April 1520. The captive Montezuma called Cortes to him, having received a report of their arrival before the captain-general did, and gave him the information, not a little smugly, saying that now he and his men could all return to their homeland across the sea, since ships to carry them had come.

The new expedition had been mounted, in white-hot fury, by the spurned Governor Velazquez of Cuba, flatly against the order of the Spanish governing council (*audiencia*) for the New World, in Santo Domingo on Hispaniola. Puertocarrero's ship, which Cortes had sent to Spain the previous summer with express orders not to stop at Cuba, had touched there nevertheless, leaving behind such tales of the treasure it was carrying that the story heard among the Spaniards in Cuba was that the ship was actually ballasted with gold. Velazquez had sent two ships in pursuit of Puertocarrero, but they failed to catch up with him. Maddened by jealousy and disappointed avarice, he bent all his efforts to raising an expedition that would bring Cortes and all his conquests and treasure under his authority. Command of the expedition was given to Panfilo de Narvaez, a tall, large-limbed man of forty-two with an imposing presence and a deep, sepulchral voice, who appears to have hardly known Cortes at all, so utterly did he underestimate him. He sent a priest, an officer, a notary, and three witnesses to demand the surrender of Veracruz. Gonzalo de Sandoval, now in command there, had them all tied up in rope hammocks and ignominiously carried to Mexico City on the backs of native porters.

But Montezuma had learned before then that the new arrivals were not friends and reinforcements of Cortes, but his enemies. Hope began to dawn in the captive emperor as he saw the terrible race of his captors preparing for civil war.

Cortes was confident that, on the strength of the victories he had already won and the treasure he had already obtained, he could win over almost all of Narvaez's army. He began with the emissaries captured by Sandoval, and soon succeeded. But this would require Cortes' personal presence with Narvaez's army, and Cortes could not risk all that might happen if he permitted that army, still under Narvaez's leadership, to march on Mexico City, in view of his very precarious situation there following the overthrow of Huitzilopochtli. It was inevitable that Cortes should choose the bolder alternative–if indeed he had a realistic choice at all.

At the beginning of May Cortes set out for the coast with almost half the men he had in Mexico City, and orders to all the rest of his men in Mexico to join him at specified points along his route of march. Eighty Spaniards were left in the capital under the command of red-haired Alvarado, along with four hundred brave Tlaxcalans, and Montezuma still their captive. The shrewd and faithful Father Olmedo was sent ahead as Cortes' personal emissary to Narvaez, to negotiate with him on the surface while telling as many of his men as possible how much more richly Cortes could and would reward those who followed him. Father Olmedo soon discovered that Narvaez had no legal right to be in Mexico at all, which no competent authority had adjudicated (or ever did adjudicate) to be under the jurisdiction of the governor of Cuba. He may also have learned that Narvaez, in threatening military action against Cortes, was directly defying the orders of the Audiencia of Santo Domingo, the highest Spanish authority in the New World, which had ordered the keeping of peace between the Spanish leaders there as the highest priority.

His position now legally and morally unassailable, Cortes proceeded at once to the attainment of his primary objective: securing the services of Narvaez's thousand men. As the knowledge of what Cortes had done in Mexico spread among these men, while Narvaez foolishly continued to hold Cortes in contempt, the willingness of his army to fight for Narvaez against Cortes declined. Cortes surprised him with an attack during a rainy night in Cempoal, which he knew like the back of his hand. Narvaez's battery of twenty-three cannon was useless in the dripping dark, his men were divided and confused as well as lacking the will to fight, and when Narvaez himself was wounded and captured, all resistance immediately collapsed. It was probably all over in an hour.

Narvaez, his deep voice unsteady but his ego as active as ever, said to the man who had beaten him: "Captain Cortes, it has been a great feat, your victory and capture of me."[73]

We can guess some of the thoughts that probably flashed through Cortes' mind on hearing that: the scuttling of his ships and the beginning here of the march inland against the overwhelming odds; the camp at the town of the hundred thousand skulls beyond the salt basin of the Mountain of the Star; the victory over the thirty thousand in Tlaxcala, against odds of a hundred to one; the carrying of the standard with the motto of Constantine over the shoulder of towering Popocatapetl and down into the keep of the Hummingbird Wizard; the capture of the Emperor of Mexico in his own palace; above all, the overthrow of the devil-gods in the great

58

temple, their replacement with an image of the Blessed Virgin Mary, and the ending of human sacrifice in Mexico City.

Hernan Cortes looked at the jealous, self-important man before him and responded with one withering sentence: "I regard it as one of the least important things I have ever done in New Spain."[74]

Back in Mexico City, it was the time of the annual festival of Toxcatl, originally a rain dance, long since taken over by the two great devil-gods, each of which was to receive a sacrificial victim specially selected for the perfection of his body. Dancing, however, continued to be a major feature of the festival, In the past Toxcatl had also been the particular occasion for the sacrifice of large numbers of captured Tlaxcalans. Montezuma had asked Cortes' permission, before he departed for the coast, to celebrate Toxcatl as usual; Cortes had agreed, except for an emphatic veto on any human sacrifice. Alvarado confirmed his agreement after Cortes' departure.

The days just before the festival, and before Cortes' victory over Narvaez, were marked by many signs of hostility of the Indians in Cactus Rock. Food supplies were no longer delivered with regularity. There were reports that the usual human sacrifices would take place at Toxcatl despite the Spanish prohibition. The Spaniards, armed and armored, came out of the palace of Axayacatl to survey the scene in the great white-stoned temple courtyard, where a new image of Huitzilopochtli was being made for the festival out of paste of amaranth seed and sticks. When the image was finished, it was clothed in a cloak painted with skulls and crossbones, and a vest "painted with dismembered human parts: skulls, ears, hearts, intestines, torsos, breasts, hands, and feet."[75] (This gruesome description comes from Aztec, not Spanish sources.) It carried a blood-red flag and shield pendant and held a flint knife steeped in human blood in its pasty hand.

Two Aztec officers now came to Alvarado and, apparently speaking for Montezuma, warned him that the Spaniards were about to be attacked and massacred. The attack could only be averted by removing the image of the Blessed Virgin Mary from the great temple and restoring an image of Huitzilopochtli there.

Alvarado, a man inferior to Cortes in intelligence and resourcefulness, but no less courageous and no less devoted to the Catholic Faith, refused, even when Montezuma confirmed the danger and the efficacy of the proposed remedy, and an attempt was actually made to remove Mary's image from the temple. But as information came to Alvarado from more and more sources that a general assault impended, and it was obvious that the Toxcatl dances would help to rouse the Aztec religious frenzy which he had already been told would be an essential motivation for the forthcoming attack, he thought of the precedent of what Cortes had done at Cholula on the way to Mexico City and resolved to repeat it at the Toxcatl festival. At the height of the wild rain-dance he and his men fell upon the dancers with all their weapons, killing hundreds. But there was a real, if rather subtle difference between this action of Alvarado's and that of Cortes at Cholula. At Cholula Cortes had solid information, confirmed just hours before through Marina, that an attack by the Indians was to be made upon his men that very day; the men he cut down had the arms in their hands with which they would have made the attack. But at the feast of Toxcatl, the rain dancers had no plans and no weapons to attack at that time. Alvarado did not know (perhaps the Aztecs themselves did not yet know) exactly when they were going to strike; and there was a distinct possibility that in fact they might not have done so.

But now, be all that as it might, the war had begun. Raging Aztecs attacked at once, driving Alvarado's Spaniards back from the temple courtyard into the palace of Axayacatl, which they had heavily fortified. Alvarado, bleeding from a head wound, confronted Montezuma, demanding that he intervene to stop the assault. Montezuma tried, but the attackers refused to listen to him any more so long as he remained a captive of the Spaniards. They were unmoved when Alvarado whipped out a dagger and held it over the emperor's heart.

For the ensuing week, while Cortes was overcoming Narvaez, the Aztecs closely besieged the Spaniards in the palace, attacking them every day. Then two brave Tlaxcalans escaped by swimming the lake on a moonless night, and loped down the trail to Cempoal to tell Cortes what had happened. He gathered all his troops, persuading the entire body of men Narvaez had brought to accompany him, and set out by forced marches for Mexico City on June 10. He now commanded over 1,300 soldiers and nearly a hundred cavalry.

He was to maintain this greatly augmented command less than three weeks.

The attack on Alvarado ceased when the news arrived that Cortes was coming. He entered Mexico City for the second time on June 24, to a deathly silence. His men in the palace of Axatacatl were safe, but they had almost no food. Montezuma told Cortes that his people would no longer obey him, or supply the Spaniards or do anything else for them. Cortes, who had been made overconfident by his spectacular victory over Narvaez, had assumed that his return would restore everything as it had been earlier in the capital and had even boasted to his new recruits about how well he was obeyed in the Aztec empire. Now no one would obey him. In his frustration and anger and his desire to justify himself to his new soldiers, Cortes even allowed himself to be outwitted for the first time by

Montezuma, who told him that if he freed his brother Cuitlahuac, who was imprisoned with him, the Aztecs would restore services to the Spaniards. Montezuma knew that was not true but hoped that Cuitlahuac would act to free him. But Cuitlahuac intended to be emperor himself. Released by Cortes, he promptly took command of the Aztec army and began drawing up the bridges in the causeways to Mexico City. The high councillors of the Aztec realm proclaimed him emperor in Montezuma's place.

On June 25 the all-out assault began. As Cortes vividly described it to King Charles:

> There came upon us from all sides such a multitude that neither the streets nor the roofs of the houses could be seen for them. They came with the most fearful cries imaginable, and so many were the stones that were hurled at us from their slings into the fortress that it seemed they were raining from the sky, and the arrows and spears were so many that all the walls and courtyards were so full we could hardly move them.[76]

The attacks went on without respite all day and all night. The palace was fired, the Spaniards putting out the conflagration only with the greatest difficulty, and Cortes was wounded by a stone which cost him for a time the use of his left hand. Had they had ten thousand Hectors and ten thousand Rolands, says Bernal Diaz, they could not have broken through that furious, screaming host. Men who had fought in Italy against the French, or in the Balkans against the Turks, said they had never seen anything like this. The Aztecs came on shouting that they would kill or capture and sacrifice every Spaniard and feed all their bodies to the jaguars, the pumas, and the snakes. Even point-blank discharges from the Spanish cannon could repel them only momentarily.

When, a day or two later, Cortes brought out Montezuma for a last appeal to what had been his people, there was in the forefront of the attackers Prince Cuauhtemoc, son of Emperor Ahuizotl who had, with Tlacaellel, presided over the dedication of the temple in 1487 with its eighty thousand human sacrifices. As Montezuma spoke, Cuauhtemoc nocked an arrow, called his uncle a Spaniard's wife, and shot. A volley of stones followed. One of them hit Montezuma squarely in the forehead. Three days later he died.

Meanwhile the attackers had reoccupied the great temple next to the palace and commanded it. Possession of the temple was the key and symbol of rule over the Aztec empire. Cortes led most of his men in an incredible sortie to regain it. Pouring out of the palace, leaving the protection of their defensive positions, the Spaniards, remembering the image of Our Lady abandoned at the top among the devils, flung themselves at the hulking structure. Cannon fire smashed the hideous skull-towers. The Spanish soldiers reached the base of the temple and began the climb. Up and up its 114 steps they fought their way. Five hundred picked warriors awaited them at the top. They pushed two forty-foot logs over the edge of the platform, but the logs turned at the last moment and slid harmlessly past the ascending Spaniards. Fifty of them, Cortes leading, reached the platform. Their fight on that commanding height which had been dedicated to evil was watched by thousands in the city. They battled their way, cut and thrust, to the chapel. The image of the Blessed Virgin Mary was gone. In her place stood the monstrous amaranth seed paste image of the Hummingbird Wizard with its vest embroidered with pieces of dismembered bodies. It was surrounded by the hearts of its latest victims–and several Spanish helmets, indicating that some of the hearts had been taken from Christians. The Spaniards hurled the images of Huitzilopochtli and Tezcatlipoca over the edge of the platform, set fire to everything on it that would burn, and fought their way down again.

"Many times I have seen paintings of this battle among the Mexicans and Tlaxcalans," says Bernal Diaz, "showing how we went up the great temple, for they look upon it as a very heroic feat."[77]

But the Aztec assaults did not abate in the slightest. Powder supplies were dwindling; food and water were almost gone. "We could see our death in our eyes," said Bernal Diaz.[78] It was decided to leave at once, on the night of the day Montezuma died, crossing the causeway to Tacuba on the far shore of Lake Texcoco. This causeway had eight bridges, all destroyed. The Spaniards had fought their way all along the causeway during the preceding day but had been unable to hold all the gaps where the bridges had been. Therefore they constructed a portable bridge for their planned escape.

Before leaving, Cortes brought out the fabulous treasure of Axayacatl which Montezuma had given them when he made his formal submission to King Charles. He carefully separated out the royal fifth and selected bearers for it. Then he told his men to take whatever they could carry of the remainder. Many, particularly the newly arrived soldiers of Narvaez, loaded themselves down with gold. Bernal Diaz, who, as he says, "had no desire but to save my life,"[79] took only four small pieces of jade.

Early in the evening the moon was out, but at ten o'clock it had begun to rain and thunder, and continued to rain throughout the night. Under this cover, at first welcome, the beleaguered Spaniards set forth after Father Olmedo said Mass, imploring God's protection in their great danger. With their portable bridge they crossed the first gap of the causeway safely. Then they were discovered. Horns blew, whistles shrilled, shouts resounded. Mexican warriors in canoes surged up on both sides of the causeway. The bridge was put down over the second gap. About half the Spaniards passed over–but not the cannon, and not the treasure for King Charles. Then the portable bridge broke in pieces under the fury of the Indian attack.

There were six more gaps in the causeway ahead, each twelve feet wide, the waters below them deeper than a man's height, though some were partially filled with rubble from the fighting along the causeway the previous day.

The main Aztec attack was made at the second gap, with its wrecked portable bridge. This was the bridge of death. Many died fighting on its canted timbers; more plunged ignominiously to the bottom of this and later gaps, weighted down by the gold they were carrying. Wrote conquistador Francisco de Aguilar forty years later, after he had been a Dominican monk for more than thirty years, of the bridge of death and what it did to the men who fought there:

> Here many Spaniards fell, some dead and some wounded, and others without any injury who fainted away from fright. And since all of us were fleeing, there was not a man who would lift a hand to help his companions or even his own father, nor a brother his own brother.[80]

There were two thousand Tlaxcalans attempting to escape with the Spaniards, altogether well over three thousand desperate men fighting and staggering and slipping and leaping down that slick rain-pelted causeway in pitch darkness lit only by the occasional wild flare of a torch and wilder flash of lightning, piling up in a human flood at each terrible gap, swept forward into it as men and horses and guns plunged or were pushed into the devouring waters. The survivors crossed the gaps only when enough bodies and baggage had accumulated in each for them to walk or wade over them with their heads still above water.

The valiant Juan Velazquez de Leon fell at the bridge of death. His was one of the bodies over which Pedro de Alvarado, one of the few survivors of the rear guard, struggled wounded, at last, to temporary safety on the far shore.

Ever afterward the Spaniards called it the Night of Sorrow. Half their army perished. The Hummingbird Wizard ruled again at Cactus Rock.

6.
Never Call Retreat
(1520-1521)

How to pick the bravest moment of that parade of superlative valor which was the conquest of Mexico? A host of occasions might contend for that honor, but none has a better claim than the deadly dawn of July 1, 1520, following the Night of Sorrow. Nearly every surviving Spaniard was wounded, and there was almost nothing with which to dress their wounds. They had nothing to eat, after having already been on the shortest of rations for an entire week. Of the twenty-four horses remaining out of eighty, not one was able to gallop. Utterly exhausted, the men could hardly even lift their arms. There were still enemies about. The Spaniards fought their way four miles farther to the Hill of the Turkey Hen, where there was a temple tower. They seized it and fortified a nearby house. There they spent the day recuperating a little, and praying for aid. Juan Rodriguez de Villafuerte left his little eleven-inch image of the Blessed Virgin Mary under a maguey plant on the hill, where it was found twenty years later and preserved in a shrine to La Virgen de los Remedios, Our Lady of Help, who became the special patron of the Spaniards in Mexico.

From the top of the temple on the Hill of the Turkey Hen they could look across the lake to Cactus Rock where, atop the great temple, those of the Spanish army who had been taken alive on the Night of Sorrow were being sacrificed, one by one, to the Hummingbird Wizard and the god of Hell.

Almost any other commander in history would, at this point, have taken the remnant of his battered and beaten army out of the country as soon and as fast as he could, boarded Narvaez's ships, and sailed for safety. But Hernan Cortes would never call retreat.

They could not stay on the Hill of the Turkey Hen, where there were no supplies. One of their faithful Tlaxcalans urged Cortes to go to his country to recover, making it a base for his return. Could Cortes trust the constancy of these Indian allies, who would have many inducements now to abandon him in his extremity? He was doubtful; but, probably thinking of their faithful service, their admiration for valor, and how much they had suffered at the hands of the Aztecs, he resolved to do so. At midnight the Spaniards set out for Tlaxcala from the Hill of the Turkey Hen, their wounded in the middle of their line of march, many still unable to walk and therefore carried lying over the backs of those horses which were themselves so lame as to be unfit to fight. With them were the dauntless Marina and two other women who had somehow survived the perils of the Night of Sorrow.

The Indians harried their march every day, making it impossible for them to gather enough provisions to appease significantly their gnawing hunger. On July 5 Cortes was hit in the head by a slingshot. Losing consciousness, he was carried to a nearby village. The Indians soon discovered the presence of the Spaniards there and attacked so fiercely that Cortes, recovering consciousness, had to get up despite his wound and lead the men with him back to the main body. The next night he ordered crutches made for the sick and wounded so that they would no longer encumber any horses, leaving all of them, even the lame, free for battle. Some Spaniards carried their comrades on their backs from time to time when they were unable to keep up; for to be left behind meant certain death on the stone of sacrifice.

On July 7, after marching some hours during the morning, the Spanish army came around the edge of a hill past the northern end of Lake Texcoco and near the ancient pyramid of Teotihuacan, and saw before them the plain of Otumba filled with an immense Indian host. New Emperor Cuitlahuac and his whole army were upon them.

It was the crisis of the conquest. Cuitlahuac and his host were between the Spaniards and Tlaxcala. Behind them was a violently hostile countryside where they could not have survived more than a few days longer. There was no way around. They had to fight their way through or perish—and not only that, but win a victory in the process, because in their condition they could not endure a vigorous pursuit by such an army. They had no guns left. All that remained of their vaunted technological superiority, to which so many later writers have attributed all their victories, were their small troop of jaded horses, a few coats of mail, and cold steel.

Says Cortes:

> There came to meet us such a multitude of Indians that the fields all around were so full of them that nothing else could be seen. We could hardly distinguish between ourselves and them, so fiercely and closely did they fight with us. Certainly we believed that it was our last day, for the Indians were very strong and we could resist but feebly, as we were exhausted and nearly all of us wounded and weak from hunger. But Our Lord was pleased to show His power and mercy, for with all our weakness we broke their arrogance and pride.[81]

Cortes halted his men at the foot of the hill. He ordered that anyone who had anything to eat should eat it. He directed that the horsemen should charge and return, again and again, at half rein. Francisco de Aguilar tells us there were tears on his cheeks; he was contemplating not only his own death and that of all the men entrusted to his care, but the ruin of all the magnificent achievements he had so recently seemed to have made, to have been crowned by the Christianization of Mexico–the triumph of the Devil, the defeat of the army of Christ. But, says Aguilar, "he drew himself up and exhorted and encouraged us like a brave captian."[82] He and his men commended their souls "to God and to Holy Mary"[83] and called upon Santiago, St. James the Greater, Apostle and Son of Thunder, the ancient patron of Spain, whom legend said had appeared in person at desperate moments of Spain's history to fight beside her Catholic soldiers when most hard beset. These men were the heirs of thirty generations of Christian warriors who had forever refused to surrender Spain to the infidel. They fought in the open now, in the glorious light of God's sunshine, far from the shadows and the deeps of the Night of Sorrow. Most of the survivors were of Cortes' original army, not of Narvaez' short-lived reinforcement. Carefree, fearless Alvarado was there, leading the cavalry charges, and thorough, relentless Sandoval, a man of indestructible hope, crying out against all odds: "Now, men, this is the day when we are going to win! Trust in God and we shall come out of this alive for some good end."[84] Dauntless, black-bearded Diego de Ordaz, the volcano climber, was there, himself a knight of Santiago, commanding the infantry. Cristobal de Olid was there, "a very Hector in combat, but his judgment was not equal to his bravery"[85] –but it was what he had, not what he lacked, that was needed this day at Otumba.

Finally Cortes called upon St. Peter, to whose special protection his parents had entrusted him thirty-four years before as a sickly baby in Extremadura, in Queen Isabel's Castile.

It was the decisive battle of the conquest. All the eight hundred years of the history of crusading Spain were needed to make men to meet the demands of this hour. No one will ever know how many Indians fought at Otumba, but in view of the fact that little Tlaxcala had fielded sixty thousand the preceding September, Lopez de Gomara's estimate of two hundred thousand at Otumba may not have been nearly so far off as many historians have tended to assume. The battle swayed to and fro. Spaniards fell; Spaniards were captured, and dragged off for sacrifice. Yet, says Bernal Diaz, "it seemed as though we all acquired double strength."[86] Cortes saw the Aztec general ahead of him, conspicuous in a huge feather crest, carrying a billowing standard. He charged. Juan de Salamanca by his side flung his lance and struck the general dead to the ground. The enemy host began to melt away. Incredible as it may seem, it was the Spaniards and their remaining Tlaxcalan allies who pursued. It was not just survival, not a draw, but a *victory*.

Cortes could now go to Tlaxcala not as a beaten commander, but as the invincible hero out of the sunrise who had triumphed once more despite all odds. It was as such that he was received. Blind old Chief Xicotencatl of Tlaxcala imprisoned his own son when he called for a rejection of the Spaniards. He and his fellow chiefs greeted Cortes with these words:

> Oh, Malinche, Malinche, how sorry we are about your misfortune and that of your brothers, and the many of our own people who have been killed along with yours! We told you many times not to trust the Mexicans, for one day or another they would attack you, but you would not believe us. Now it has happened and no more can be done at present but to attend you and give you food. You are at home; rest, and soon we will go to our town and put you up. Do not think, Malinche, that it was a little thing to escape with your lives from that strong city with its bridges. I tell you that if before we took you to be very brave, now we take you to be much more so. It is true that many of the women and girls in our town weep for their sons and husbands, brothers and relatives, but do not grieve for that. You owe much to your gods, who have brought you here and delivered you from such a multitude of warriors as were waiting for you at Otumba.[87]

In his Tlaxcalan refuge Cortes began, with hardly a pause, to plan for his victorious return to Mexico City. It never occurred to him that he was starting (as many modern writers seem to regard him as having started) a new, aggressive war by continuing the one begun in Mexico City and so vigorously extended by the Aztecs through the Battle of Otumba. He and his men had been guests in Mexico City, where Emperor Montezuma had sworn allegiance to King Charles. Cortes had taken action to enforce the laws of King Charles against human sacrifice and idolatry. The Aztecs had demanded his departure, plotted to kill him and his men, and finally attacked and killed half of them. He was now returning to punish them as conquer. The fact that the Aztecs would have found certain steps in this chain of reasoning and justification difficult to follow does not prove that chain to have been either erroneous or hypocritical. The enthusiastic adhesion of the Tlaxcalans is enough to show that this was no ethnic war for liberty from an alien invader, but at least as much a war of liberation against the fiendishly totalitarian empire of the Aztecs.

To destroy that empire and establish Christian dominion over the Valley of Mexico, Cortes needed, first, to restore the shaken morale of this men by maintaining them successfully in Tlaxcala and securing nearby regions; then to regain the initiative in the central lake region itself; finally, to develop a means of penetrating and remaining in Mexico City that would not lead to another Night of Sorrow. Tlaxcalan constancy and Spanish valor would soon provide the first two requirements; Cortes decided to meet the third by the construction of a lake fleet of brigantines capable of controlling the waters adjacent to the causeways leading to the capital. He sent trusty Gonzalo de Sandoval to Veracruz to make sure of the Spanish hold on the coast and round up as reinforcements all Spaniards and Spanish military supplies which he found there, while Cortes himself campaigned to secure the route from Veracruz to Tlaxcala. By the end of the year 1520 Cortes was firmly in command of all central Mexico from Popcatapetl to the sea, and the assembly of ship timbers for his brigantines had begun in dry but secure Tlaxcala.

Just after Christmas 1520 the recuperated, reinforced and reinvigorated Spanish army set out from Tlaxcala, bound once again for Mexico City. They were now six hundred strong, with forty horses and nine cannons. As before, they took the worst road past the volcanoes, despite its blockage by great tree trunks and the biting cold of the great heights. Cortes rode in the very forefront of the army with only four companions. When they reached the first point from which the whole valley and the great lake could be clearly seen, Cortes assembled the army. He called on them to give thanks to God for having preserved their lives and brought them back this far in safety. He added, in his third letter to King Charles, whom he now knew to be Emperor Charles V:

> From there we could see before us the province of Mexico and Temixtitan [Tenochtitlan], which lies in the lakes and by their shore. Although we were greatly pleased to see it, recollecting how much harm we had suffered there, we were somewhat sad and all swore never to leave the province alive if we did not do so victorious. And with this resolution we moved on as joyfully as if we were on an outing.[88]

Cortes descended with his army from the heights to the valley floor and the lake at Texcoco in the middle of the eastern shore, which he promptly occupied as many of the inhabitants evacuated it. Here he planned to assemble and launch the brigantines now under construction in Tlaxcala.

The reappearance of Cortes with a reinforced army renewed in resolution must have been a tremendous shock to the Aztecs, though nothing could now shake the determination of the majority of their aristocracy to fight the Spaniards to the death. During the preceding fall Mexico had been ravaged by a devastating smallpox epidemic, a disease brought by the invader to which the Indians had no developed immunity or natural defenses. (To make this smallpox epidemic primarily responsible for Cortes' recovery and victory, as some writers do, is not only to overlook the still remaining immense disparity in numbers between the Aztecs and the invaders, but also the fact that Cortes' allies in Tlaxcala were equally susceptible to smallpox and equally stricken by it, yet still put tens of thousands of their warriors into the field to help him.) New Emperor Cuitlahuac was one of the victims of the plague, along with the strongly pro-Spanish war leader Chief Maxixcatzin of Tlaxcala. But Maxixcatzin was replaced by an equally brave and pro-Spanish commander, Chichimecatecle, while Cuitlahuac's successor was the fanatical Cuauhtemoc, who had led the attack that killed his own uncle and ruler, Montezuma. The towns of Otumba, on the east side of the lake where the great battle had been fought, and rich Chalco at the southeast corner, both submitted to the Spaniards. Cuauhtemoc in a fury sent a large army to try to regain Chalco. After it was repulsed by an expeditionary force headed by Sandoval, several Aztec officers captured in this engagement were sent to Cuauhtemoc with a message from Cortes,

> that he did not wish to be the cause of the King's [Cuauhtemoc's] downfall or of that of his great city, and that if they came in peace he would pardon them for the deaths and damage they had inflicted on us and would demand nothing whatever of them, but to take care, for war was easy to stop at its beginning, but difficult afterward, and it would end in their destruction. How could he wish to see his city destroyed and all his people killed? He should consider the great power of Our Lord God, in Whom we believed and Whom we worshiped, for He always helped us.[89]

Cuauhtemoc's only response was to send to all the provinces that still obeyed him an order that any Spaniard taken prisoner should be brought at once to Mexico City for sacrifice at the great temple. That order was carefully and conscientiously carried out right up to the final moments of the fall of the city and the temple.

In the latter part of February 1521 an immense procession of 8,000 Tlaxcalan bearers and 20,000 escorting Tlaxcalan soldiers, along with a Spanish detachment under Sandoval, wound its way into Texcoco for no less than six hours, carrying all the parts for thirteen brigantines which were now to be assembled there. At almost the same time three ships arrived in Veracruz, having come directly from Spain via Santo Domingo, probably in response to the news of Cortes' discoveries and achievements in Mexico. They brought a Franciscan friar from Seville carrying bulls of indulgence for men fighting on crusade, a royal treasurer, and further reinforcements amounting to no less than 350 infantry and forty-six cavalry.

Once these strong new forces were brought up, Cortes took three hundred infantry and twenty cavalry, along with a considerable number of the best Tlaxcalan warriors, on his most ambitious campaign since the Night of Sorrow. Its mission was nothing less than a complete fighting circuit of the central lake of Mexico to demonstrate the closing of the Spanish armed ring about the capital. There were fierce and furious engagements on the road to Cuernavaca and back to Xochimilco of the floating gardens, on the lake. The Aztecs defended Xochimilco in great strength and with desperate determination, while the Spaniards and their horses, on their first approach to it, were weakened by a long march from Cuernavaca without water. Cortes' horse fell in the midst of the enemy. Some of the attackers, recognizing him, rushed to capture him. His life was saved by a heroic but nameless Tlaxcalan and by the valiant Cristobal de Olea of Bernal Diaz's home town of Medina del Campo, who held off the enemy by a magnificent display of swordsmanship while suffering three severe wounds. Bernal Diaz and a few others heard the shouting and rushed to aid in the rescue of Cortes, taking him back to a walled enclosure for protection. The Aztecs, knowing that the capture of Cortes could change the whole course of the war, launched a massive, screaming attack on the improvised defensive position, which was little more than an enclosed courtyard or patio. Their initial assault wounded many of the defenders; but these were veterans of the first march inland, survivors of the Night of Sorrow, victors of Otumba. Says Bernal Diaz of the attackers:

> They didn't come on very well, for we quickly gave them their fill with good swordplay, and the horsemen wasted no time before attacking, and they killed many. Two horses were wounded, but we drove them out of the place.[90]

The battle of Xochimilco, a foretaste of the later struggle for Mexico City, lasted three full days and ended with the beautiful town, built partly on water like the capital, an utter ruin. At the end of that week in April 1521, Cortes and his men reached Tacuba, from which ran the causeway to Mexico City over which the remnant had escaped on the Night of Sorrow. Cortes climbed to the top of the temple in Tacuba and looked across the lake to Cactus Rock, to the forbidding specter of the great temple, to the palace of Axayacatl where the Spaniards had been welcomed by Montezuma as honored guests, and then fought desperately for their lives. Bernal Diaz writes memorably of Cortes' reaction:

> At this sight Cortes gave a long, sad sigh, much greater than any before, for the men who had been killed. It was on this that the romance or song was written beginning:
> In Tacuba was Cortes, with many a gallant chief,
> He thought about his losses and bowed his head in grief.

I recall that one of our soldiers, Alonzo Perez, who resided in Mexico after the conquest, said to Cortes, "Señor Captain, do not be sad, for those things always happen in war. You are not to be compared with Nero watching Rome burn."[91]

It is likely that Cortes was thinking not only of his past losses, but of the devastation to come; for the tenacity and fervor of the Aztec resistance, even in the face of steadily growing Spanish strength, was rapidly increasing the likelihood that the price of the conquest of Mexico City would be its total destruction. When the Spaniards had first marched into it, across the causeways, it had seemed a city materialized from a dream, of breathtaking beauty and unlimited promise. They knew the dark shadow which dwelt at its heart, but had believed they could cleanse it, cut it out by deft surgery. But the scalpel had failed; now was the time of battle-axe and mace. Cactus Rock would vanish from the face of the earth, never to return. Said Cortes to Emperor Charles V:

They gave us cause, and indeed obliged us, to destroy them utterly. On this last I dwelt with more sorrow, for it weighed heavily on my soul.[92]

7.
The Wizard Dethroned
(1521)

Cuauhtemoc had decided upon war to the death; and he was dealing with men who knew exactly what that meant and would give it to him if he asked for it. As Burr C. Brundage says in his history of the Aztecs:

> The siege of the city of Mexico is one of the most savage and desperate encounters in all history. It is heroic in the classical mode and hopeless at the same time. The enemy's policy of calculated terror and total destruction caused the city to melt away before the defenders' eyes, so that it became in its desolation much like the original mud flat of the founding days. One source says that 100,000 Mexicans and close allies were killed and drowned in the siege, with as many again dying of starvation, dysentery, and other diseases. The Tlatilulca remembered their city at the end in the following terms: "In the streets lay broken bones and torn out hanks of hair. Houses had fallen apart; they lay open with their walls spattered with blood. Worms wriggled in the cluttered streets. Walls were dirtied with bits of brains. The water was dyed with blood. Even so we drank it. We drank it with salty blood."[93]

War is organized horror; and few wars have been more horrible than this. Brundage's unforgettable picture portrays no more and no worse than the truth. But what it does not say is that Cortes offered Cuauhtemoc peace, again and again, up to the very last moments of the struggle; and there is good reason to believe that more than once, toward the end, Cuauhtemoc wanted to accept his offers. But the Hummingbird Wizard would not let him. Each time its priests ordered Cuauhtemoc unequivocally to make no peace with the Christians. Cortes had long known the ultimate enemy he faced in Mexico; it is likely that he foresaw something like this when he gave his long sigh on beholding Mexico City from the temple top in Tacuba, and was consoled by kindly Alonzo Perez. For whatever future Tenochtitlan might have had, whatever conditions of peace Cortes might ultimately have offered, one thing was certain: the Hummingbird Wizard would be forever dethroned by Cortes' victory. There would be no more living human hearts torn out at Cactus Rock, when the Spaniards had won it this time. And so the heirs of Tlacaellel and the acolytes of

Satan would go down fighting, dragging the whole of what had been their city with them.

On Sunday, April 28, 1521, Father Olmedo said Mass to dedicate the fleet, and the thirteen brigantines, bedecked with flags, each manned by twenty-five Spaniards, were launched upon the lake. Almost a thousand Spaniards and more than 75,000 Indian allies were ready for the final campaign. On May 13 they set out from Texcoco to take up positions at the entrances to the causeways leading to Mexico City. It was the beginning of ninety-three consecutive days of incessant, unrelenting warfare.

The task confronting Cortes would have been formidable enough against any resolute enemy. Against hundreds of thousands of foes imbued with fanatical passion and the wild energy of a berserk despair, it seemed almost beyond human power for his small force to accomplish. Three causeways led to Mexico City: the largest from the south, Y-shaped, with one leg of the Y extending from Coyoacan and the other from Iztapalapa, crossing the islet of Acachinanco after they joined–the causeway on which the Spaniards had first entered the city; the second from Tacuba to the west, across which the Spanish remnant had escaped on the Night of Sorrow; the third from the hill of Tepeyac to the north, where Our Lady of Guadalupe was later to appear. Cortes commanded the largest force, attacking up the southern causeway; Alvarado commanded the force attacking over the western or Tacuba causeway; Sandoval commanded the force attacking down the northern or Tepeyac causeway. Attacks along these causeways were possible only because of the presence of the Spanish brigantines to fend off flank attacks by Aztec warriors in their innumerable canoes. But to do this, the brigantines had to maneuver in very confined waters which were made constantly hazardous by the planting of underwater obstacles, primarily pointed stakes. This made it almost impossible for the brigantines to operate at night. Therefore every daylight advance of the Spaniards along the causeways and across the deadly gaps which had cost them so much on the Night of Sorrow, was followed by a night of retreat and destruction in which most of what they had gained during the day was lost again. Gaps they had filled in were opened up again by the defenders. On the next day most or all of the victories of the preceding day had to be won again.

Cuauhtemoc and his generals were confident that by such tactics they would wear down, discourage, and ultimately repulse even such persistent and well-equipped foes. Nor was their expectation unreasonable. Few troops of any nation, at any point in history, could have stood up to the demands and the cost and the apparent futility of that endless daily hammering, against an apparently indestructible opponent, for more than three months. It was in this way like the campaign of Spotsylvania and the Wilderness in the American Civil War, or the Battle of Guadalcanal in World War II–but essentially worse than either of these, for in the assault on Mexico City any Spaniard who fell into the hands of the enemy knew with a grim and total certainty that his still living heart would be ripped from his chest and his body eaten by his captors and their animals. Yet no more than their captain-general would any of the Spaniards now call retreat. "Not one but many times the Spaniards declared," says Cortes, "that they asked of God only that they should live to triumph over the defenders of the city, even if this should mean that they gained nothing else in the entire land."[94] But Bernal Diaz, as always, put it best:

> When I saw my companions sacrificed, their hearts taken out still beating, their arms and legs cut off, I was truly afraid that one day it might happen to me. They had already seized me twice to take me to be sacrifice, and it pleased God that I escaped from them, but ever since then I feared death more than ever. Before going into battle a kind of terror gripped me. But then when I went into battle, commending myself to God and His Blessed Mother, the fear left me.[95]

By June 9 Cortes and his men had smashed and battered their way right up to the center of the city, to the palace of Axayacatl where they had stayed as guests of Montezuma, and to the great temple. The palace was set on fire and burned to the ground, along with many of the zoo buildings and other structures. Once again Cortes fought his way up the 114 punishing steps to the top of the great temple, where he also fired the new wooden image of the Hummingbird Wizard which had been set up there. But as usual, the triumph was only for the day. The Spaniards dared not remain in the city at night because of the myriad of relentlessly attacking enemies, but instead withdrew across the causeways to secure quarters. When they returned to action at the first light of dawn, after hearing Mass, they found the gaps in the causeway so much opened again and so well defended that they expended almost all their available ammunition in a five-hour battle to cross the first two of the three gaps between their night quarters and the temple square–which they never did regain that day, nor for many days thereafter.

On June 20, 1521, the first anniversary of the Night of Sorrow, the Spaniards, goading each other on with the overflowing vehemence of their commitment to victory despite all obstacles, by their insistence committed their commander to a new general assault on the market-place of Tlatelolco, which Bernal Diaz had visited that very first Sunday in Mexico City, and the which had not yet been reached by the Spaniards in any of the attacks of the great siege. Somehow the impression had taken hold of their minds that if only they could seize this market-place, victory would be assured. Charging furiously and without sufficient care for their line of retreat, the attackers from the south under Cortes were cut off by the breaking of a causeway gap in their rear. As they began to fall back in disorder, the Indians actually plunging into the waters of the gap on top of the Spaniards to kill or capture them, Cortes and some dozen heroes rushed to help their struggling, drowning comrades. In a few minutes they were surrounded by an Indian multitude, including some officers who recognized their chief enemy "Malinche" and were determined to capture him for sacrifice. They wounded him in the leg and laid hold of him to drag him away. The intrepid Christobal de Olea, who had saved Cortes' life at Xochimilco, once again rushed into the fray for this same purpose, with sword swinging, alone. He went down fighting, giving his life that his commander might live–Bernal Diaz's fellow townsman, clear-voiced and handsome, twenty-six years old, born under the great Queen Isabel about the time Columbus set out on his second voyage to America. Cortes wanted to fight on; but Captain Antonio de Quinones came up, seized his arm, and pulled him away, crying: "Save at least your own person, for you know that if you are killed we are all lost."[96]

The survivors struggled to safety at last; the Aztecs flung severed Spanish heads at each retreating column–Cortes', Alvarado's, Sandoval's–shouting that the commanders of the other columns were killed and the Spanish decisively defeated. In fact, some seventy Spanish prisoners were taken that day. The next day, to the sepulchral boom of the great snakeskin drum that sounded as though it came from the very bottom of Hell, the first of them were forced to dance naked before the Hummingbird Wizard on the top of the great temple, sacrificed, flayed, and dismembered, all in full view of the other Spanish soldiers, helpless to stop it and save them. Many of their Indian allies, deeply discouraged by this setback and alarmed by a prophecy of the priests of Huitzilopochtli that Cortes would be destroyed while Venus, Quetzalcoatl's and therfore Cortes' star, was in conjunction with the sun and therefore invisible for eight days, withdrew for the time being from the besieging army.

But several of the most tenacious and pro-Spanish allied chiefs remained, notably Ixtilxochitl of Texcoco, who had been baptized as Carlos. He urged the Spaniards to take the eight days of the prophecy to recuperate, concentrating their military efforts on action by the brigantines more effectively to cut off the supply of food and especially of water to the defenders. For Lake Texcoco was salt, and at the beginning of the siege the Spaniards had cut the aqueducts to the capital city from Chapultepec. The thousands of defenders were subsisting on a few brackish wells, occasional boatloads of water brought out from the shore, and collected rainwater. It had been barely enough. Any interference with their water supplies brought by boat would soon create a crisis of thirst.

The eight days passed; the last Spaniards captured in the defeat of June 30 were sacrificed; but Cortes was still there. He sent expeditions to protect his Indian allies despite the temporary desertion of many of them, and to scatter would-be relieving forces. Soon his allies, their confidence in him renewed, were streaming back into camp. Cortes now made repeated appeals to the defenders, whose last rational hope had gone, to surrender or at least to negotiate; but they refused to consider any terms but the complete departure of all Spaniards from the land. Bernal Diaz remembered their shouting:

> Why does Malinche come every day asking peace with us? Our idols have promised us victory, and we have plenty of water and provisions! We will leave none of you alive! Don't talk any more about peace. Words are for women–arms for the men![97]

So, with a heavy heart, in the third week of July 1521, Cortes gave the order to his now enormous army–including nearly 150,00 Indian allies along with the thousand Spaniards–to press on into the city destroying every house as they advanced and killing every man they found who would not surrender. Soon he was horrified to learn that his allies, who after all were of the same culture and religion as the Aztecs and had suffered bitter wrongs at their hands for generations, would not now take any prisoners at all–neither men, nor women, nor children. The Spanish soldiers saved the women and children wherever they could. But over most of Cactus Rock, during that last fell month of the great siege, death reigned, and nothing but death.

About the beginning of August the slowly advancing Spaniards reached the two great temples, this time to stay. Cortes in person commanded the successful assault on the market-place and temple of Tlatelolco, the section of the city where resistance had for some time been the strongest. Climbing to the top of the temple, he could see that seven-eighths of the city was now in the hands of his men. Meanwhile his countryman, sturdy Gutierre of Badajoz in Extremadura, was leading the last assault up the 114 steps of the great temple of the Hummingbird Wizard, the priests fighting step by step as they always did. When the attackers gained the top they put everything to the torch, so that the licking flames and billowing smoke could be seen all across the city. Looking over from the temple top at Tlatelolco, Cortes saw the smoke-pyre. He had always known his real enemy in Mexico. Turning to the men with him, he said–and we can almost see the steely flash in his eyes–that he wished he were there.

The Hummingbird Wizard was dethroned at last, this time forever, in Cactus Rock.

On August 13, 1521, still refusing to hear any talk of peace, Cuauhtemoc, who for some days had been living in and ruling from a canoe because he no longer held any building which could be regarded as secure, was captured in the lake by a brigantine commanded by Garcia Holguin, who brought him immediately to Cortes. The last emperor of the Aztecs, who seems to have known in his heart during the last weeks that continued resistance in his hopeless cause was irrational and evil, said to his conqueror, with tears streaming down his cheeks: "Take that dagger from your belt and kill me with it quickly."[98]

Cortes refused, speaking to him kindly and with respect, yet also with profound regret for all the death and destruction that had come from the unnecessary prolongation of the struggle. The days of automatic slaying of defeated leaders had ended in Mexico, which henceforth was to belong to Christ and His Mother.

A vast, incredible silence fell. Let Bernal Diaz describe it:

> All of us soldiers were as deaf as though up to now we had been in a bell tower with all the bells ringing. For the ninety-three days of the siege there had been constant cries and whistles day and night, the shouts of Mexican captains giving orders on the causeways, others crying to the canoes, putting in palisades and marine barricades. In addition to all this their accursed drums and horns never stopped sounding from their towers and oratories, so that it was impossible to hear anyone talk. Now that Guatemuz [Cuauhtemoc] was captured, all the noise and voices stopped.[99]

Part II
The Spiritual Conquest of Mexico

8.
Twelve Poor Men
(1521-1527)

To cut great evil by the sword, necessary and even magnificently heroic though it may be, does not automatically ensure the triumph of the good. Christianity is not gained or maintained by force, but by grace and the Cross, by holiness. Christianity could never have coexisted with Tlacaellel's Mexico. But to build Christendom on the ashes and the ruins of Tlacaellel's Mexico required a spiritual splendor and heroism of a wholly different order from the heroism that had overthrown the Hummingbird Wizard.

It was not reasonable to expect most of the original conquerors to play a major role in the spiritual conquest of Mexico. All too often they have been self-righteously condemned by writers who seem to think that most of them should have been monks (though a few of them, like Francisco de Aguilar, did in fact become exactly that). They knew better. Cortes himself had told Montezuma that in times to come "our lord and king would send men who lead holy lives, better than ourselves, who would explain everything [about the Christian Faith], for we had come only to notify them."[100] Bernal Diaz had simply said, in final comment on his commander's life and his own: "God pardon him his sins and me mine."[101] These were men whose spiritual humility ought to shame their critics.

It is the greatest of all the glories of Spain in its golden age that it produced, and knew how to recognize and to honor, not only conquistadors, but saints.

Yet the spiritual conquest of Mexico, as it now lay before its conquerors, was a task too great even for saints to accomplish quickly. Perhaps as many as twenty million people lived in a rugged, much-broken land of great variation in elevation, topography, and climate, in which no less than 114 separate languages were spoken, 51 of which were sufficiently widespread and became well enough known to be written down and later to be classified linguistically. The Nahuatl language of the Aztec empire was the most widespread and was known to many as a second language; but there were still millions of Indians who did not know it or knew only a few words of it. Whatever the virtues of the missionaries or the prestige of the conquerors (who at no time forced baptism on any significant number of Indians), the sheer physical difficulties of reaching so many fundamentally alien people, never having had the slightest previous contact with Christianity or with any aspect of Christian civilization, were overwhelming. In similar missionary situations which the Iberian peoples later confronted elsewhere in the world, in which evangelization was carried on no less zealously than in Mexico, it required three hundred years for the Portuguese to convert half the population of Angola in Africa, and two hundred years for the Spanish to convert much of the population of the Philippines. Even in Peru the conversion required a full century.

But when Bernal Diaz was writing his vivid, unforgettable narrative of the conquest of Mexico, fifty years after it began, the conversion of Mexico was not only complete, but had been established long enough to bear fruit in a truly Christian culture. All the Indians he knew and saw had become Christians, confessing their sins every year, frequently attending Mass.

It is a thing worthy to thank God on to see the devotion which the natives exhibit when at holy Mass, especially if it is said by fathers of the orders of St. Francis, or of Mercy who are appointed to the cures of parishes. All the natives also, men, women, and children are taught the holy prayers in their mother tongue, and when they pass a cross, crucifix, or altar, they bow, falling on their knees to say a Pater Noster or Ave Maria. . . . On the day of Our Lady, or of Corpus Christi, and other solemn feasts, when we make processions, most of the neighbors of this city of Guatemala go in procession with crosses and lighted candles, bearing the image of the saint who is their patron or patroness, as richly dressed as they can afford; and they go singing the litanies, and other holy prayers, and sound their flutes and trumpets.[102]

In one climactic paragraph, Bernal Diaz sums up his own life and achievement, and far beyond that, the victory God won in Mexico and the part His Mother played in it.

Consider the number of cities of New Spain, which from their being so many, I will not detail; our ten bishoprics, not including the archbishopric of the noble city of Mexico, the three courts of royal audience, together with the succession of governors, archbishops and bishops, our holy cathedrals and monasteries, Dominican,

Franciscan, Mercedarian, and Augustinian, our hospitals with the extensive remissions and pardons attached to them, and the Santa Casa [Shrine] of Our Lady of Guadalupe with the holy miracles there performed every day, and let us give thanks to God, and to His blessed mother Our Lady, for giving us grace and support to conquer these countries, where so much Christianity is now established.[103]

This miraculous conversion, for which Cortes' conquistadors had opened the way, began primarily with twelve poor men.

The news of Cortes' gigantic achievement had reached Spain half-hidden in smoke of calumny generated by the envious and the avaricious, who either resented his success, or wished to profit from it without taking the risks he had taken and enduring the hardships he had endured. Charles V, the grandson of Queen Isabel, a great and much misunderstood and unappreciated monarch who had more than a little similarity to Cortes himself, was only temporarily misled by the cloud of accusations. He returned to Spain in July 1522 after an absence of more than two years, during which he had assumed the title and mission of Holy Roman Emperor, temporal protector of Christendom from the infidel without and the heretic within, and had told Martin Luther to his face that all his dominions, his body, his blood, his life, and his soul were committed to the preservation of the Catholic Faith. One of Charles' first acts upon his return to Spain was to appoint a commission to review the evidence on what had happened in Mexico and make a recommendation in favor of either Velazquez of Cuba, or Cortes. The commission found for Cortes, and in October Charles V officially recognized him as governor and Captain-General of New Spain (Cortes' name for Mexico) and wrote him a personal letter warmly thanking him for his great services. In June 1523 he wrote to Cortes again, particularly emphasizing his obligation to convert the Indians of Mexico and end all human sacrifice, cannibalism, and idolatry there.

Meanwhile a leading Spanish Franciscan, Fray Francisco de los Angeles of the Quinones family, had offered himself and a Flemish Franciscan, Juan Glapion, to go to Mexico to work for the evangelization of its people, almost as soon as he heard of Cortes' arrival there. Pope Leo X gave his approval April 25, 1521, just three days before Cortes launched his brigantines for the final assault on Mexico City. However, Father Glapion died soon afterwards, as did Pope Leo himself, and Francisco de los Angeles was becoming so prominent in his order that it was difficult for him to leave Europe. In May 1522 the new Pope, Adrian VI (a Netherlander, who had been the tutor of Emperor Charles V as a boy, and was the last non-Italian Pope before John Paul II) issued a bull authorizing any members of the mendicant orders designated by their superiors to go to the New World to assist in the conversion of the Indians. Three Flemish Franciscans, two priests and a lay brother, sailed almost immediately afterwards; two priests soon died, but the lay brother, Peter of Ghent, worked many years among the Indians and became famous throughout Mexico. Francisco de los Angeles was elected general of the Franciscan order in 1523; but, retaining his deep interest in a Mexican mission, he made one of the first tasks in his new office the selection for that mission of a superior, or guardian, with twelve friars under him. His choice was Martin of Valencia, provincial of San Gabriel and founder of the monastery of Santa Maria del Berrocal, a man with a reputation for great holiness, forty-nine years old, born in the year Isabel was crowned Queen of Castile. In October 1523 Fray Martin received his instructions, and toward the end of the year his twelve met together for the first time at the monastery of Santa Maria de Belvis. Ten were priests, six of whom were known as learned men and great preachers; two were lay brothers.

How much they then knew of Mexico we cannot be sure, but enough information had accumulated in Spain by the end of 1523, including the first three of the remarkably vivid and detailed letters of Cortes himself, so that they must have had at least the beginnings of comprehension of the magnitude of the task before them. From the facts we have, we can sense their eagerness and zeal; for their official instructions were issued in October, the twelve met with Fray Martin at Belvis monastery in November or December, and by January they were at sea (all but one who was unavoidably detained), crossing to Santo Domingo on Hispaniola by the fast trade-wind route. They arrived in time for Easter 1524, stayed in Santo Domingo to celebrate it, then sailed on to Mexico. On Friday, May 13, they landed in Veracruz. Gonzalo de Sandoval, Cortes' most trusted lieutenant, met them as they disembarked, standing as official witness for the receipt of their documents of authorization. As soon as Cortes heard of their arrival, he sent Juan de Villagomez from Mexico City to do everything possible to help and honor them.

But these men, sons of St. Francis following in the footsteps of the first Twelve Apostles, would accept no comforts. Christians had now been in this land five years; Fray Martin and his companions would have been morally certain that the avarice and gold hunger of some of the Spaniards had already given grave scandal to those they hoped to convert. Here is one Aztec description of Spaniards catching sight of gold:

> They gave the "gods" ensigns of gold, and ensigns of quetzal feathers, and golden necklaces. And when they were given those presents, the Spaniards burst into smiles, their eyes shone with

pleasure; they were delighted by them. They picked up the gold and fingered it like monkeys; they seemed to be transported by joy, as if their hearts were illumined and made new.

The truth is that they longed and lusted for gold. Their bodies swelled with greed, and their hunger was ravenous; they hungered like pigs for that gold.[104]

When they were ready to go inland, Martin of Valencia and his eleven Franciscan apostles set out on the 200-mile journey to Mexico City, across mountains and deserts, in thin brown habits, *barefoot*.

For the next two hundred and fifty years, every Franciscan missionary entering Mexico for the first time walked the 200 miles from Veracruz to Mexico City barefoot. It was done when Fray Junipero Serra, the apostle of California, arrived in the eighteenth century.

When they reached Tlaxcala thousands of Indians gathered to see them, along with the Spaniards whom Cortes had instructed to greet them with every honor, chiefly the ringing of the bells which almost every village already had. The friars marvelled at the numbers to be evangelized and praised God for providing them with the opportunity to help win so many souls for Him. Unable as yet to speak a word of any Indian language, they could only point again and again to the sky, hoping that some at least of the Indians would understand that it was into all the glory and loftiness symbolized by the sky, to the true Heaven, that the new faith they came to preach would lead these people.

Astounded at the contrast between the friars and most other Spaniards they had known, the Indians kept crying out, *"Motolinea! Motolinea!"* One of the friars, Toribio de Benavente, asked a Spanish soldier what the word meant. "Poor," was the reply, "poor fellow." "Then that will be my name for the rest of my life,"[105] said Fray Toribio; and so he is known to history and literature as Toribio Motolinea, author of the first great religious history of New Spain and account of its native people.

When the twelve, dusty, ragged and still barefoot, reached Mexico City, Cortes himself came out to meet them at the shore of the lake, with Cuauhtemoc and many Aztec and Spanish noblemen. Cortes knelt and tried to kiss Fray Martin's hand. When, out of humility, the friar refused, Cortes kissed his habit.

The Spanish historian Mendieta calls it the "highest [deed] Cortes ever did."[106]

Contemplating the immensity of their task, the twelve immediately began a fifteen-day retreat of prayer and penance, joined by the Flemish Franciscans already in Mexico. On July 2, when the retreat ended, they held a chapter meeting. Fray Martin was confirmed as superior despite his protests, and it was decided to establish four separate houses at once: one in Mexico City itself, a second at Texcoco on the eastern shore of the lake, a third in Tlaxcala, and a fourth in Huejotzingo between Tlaxcaca and Cholula. This would concentrate their efforts in the central capital region and in Tlaxcala, whose alliance with the Spaniards during the conquest and particularly warm welcome for the friars promised well for the work of evangelization.

Within six months several of the friars, totally immersing themselves in the life of the Indians, and with the aid of Cortes' original Spanish interpreter Jeronimo de Aguilar, were able to understand and make themselves understood in Nahuatl, so that in the course of 1525 actual preaching and instruction could begin without dependence on scarce and often undesirable interpreters. The most famous of the early Franciscan scholars in Mexico, Fray Bernardino de Sahagun, preserved actual copies of some of the first sermons on the Christian faith preached to the chiefs and even to the pagan priests of Mexico by some of these twelve Franciscans, as their essential instruction before baptism.

> You have a god, you say, whose worship has been taught to you by your ancestors and your kings. Not so! You have a multitude of gods, each with his function. . . . And what they demand of you in sacrifice is your blood, your heart. Their images are loathsome. On the other hand . . . the true and universal God, Our Lord, Creator and Dispenser of being and life, as we have been telling you in our sermons, had a character different from that of your gods. He does not deceive; He dies not; He hates no one, despises no one; there is nothing evil in Him. He regards all wickedness with the greatest horror, forbids and interdicts it, for He is perfectly good. He is the deep well of all good things; He is the essence of love, compassion, and mercy. And He showed His infinite mercy when He made Himself Man here on earth, like us; humble and poor, like us. He died for us and spilled His Precious Blood to redeem us and free us from the power of evil spirits. This true God is called Jesus Christ, true God and true Man, Dispenser of being and life, Redeemer and Savior of the world.[107]

But the twelve poor Franciscans, being what they were, would not confine their evangelization to those of higher rank. From the beginning they went also to the *macehualtin*, the poor of God. Motolinea's history tells us that the first two villages evangelized from the Franciscan house in Mexico City were Cuauhtitlan and Tepotzotlan, on the western shore of the lake.

In Cuauhtitlan lived quietly, unknown, the humble maker of reed mats named Cuauhtlatohuac, "He who talks like an eagle," now in his late forties, who had been just thirteen when Tlacaellel had the eighty thousand men sacrificed at the dedication of the great temple to the Hummingbird Wizard in Mexico City. It was at this time, in the year 1525, that he was converted and baptized Juan Diego, very probably by one of Fray Martin's twelve poor men.

Meanwhile, the men who had dethroned the Hummingbird Wizard were being taught again one of the world's hardest, oldest lessons for the Christian: that Satan is immortal.

At the beginning of 1524 Cortes had sent his least capable and least trustworthy lieutenant, Cristobal de Olid, he of the great bravery and the bad judgment, with six ships and four hundred men for the conquest of Honduras in Central America. (Alvarado was sent at the same time to conquer Guatemala, which he accomplished promptly and with little bloodshed.) Olid found little in Honduras to conquer, but at so great a distance from his superior officer, far away by sea around the great bulge of the Yucatan peninsula, he decided to throw off Cortes' authority and rule what was there on his own. Such rebellion was common among the conquistadors in the early years of the Spanish expansion; Velazquez of Cuba had always considered Cortes himself guilty of it, though he had taken care to justify his position under Spanish law and by regular communication with the king–scruples which Olid scorned. But Cortes resented it out of all reason. Instead of ignoring Olid (who really wanted Honduras anyway?), or appealing to Emperor Charles V, or sending a more loyal officer against him, Cortes made what his biographer Salvador de Madariaga rightly calls "the most tragic mistake of his life."[108]

He decided to go to Honduras in person, with many of his best and most loyal officers, by land, though he did not know the road. And no man knew the road–because there was no road.

Look at a modern map of southern Mexico and Guatemala, working south from the jungles of Tabasco through the drowned lowlands of the Usumacinta River and past Lake Peten in northeastern Guatemala to the jagged rock spine of the Santa Cruz Mountains, which become the Cockscombs in Belize. To this day most of it is untouched by railroad or road. Just a few years ago the first highway in Mexican history was driven across the lower Usumacinta at enormous cost and after years of effort. Most of the region remains, as it was in 1524, impassable.

Cortes and his veterans of the campaign against odds of ten thousand to one–Sandoval was with him, and Bernal Diaz, and many others–passed it. No other army ever had, or probably ever will, or perhaps ever could have. It took even the heroes of the conquest *eight full months*, during most of which they were on the verge of starvation and totally cut off from the world. More than once they had to build bridges a mile long. Cortes took Cuauhtemoc with him and had him executed on the way when he believed the former Aztec emperor was planning to use his desperate situation to destroy him. With an imprudence inexplicable in such a man, Cortes left behind him in Mexico City not one governor, but *four*: Estrada, Albornoz, Salazar, and Chirino. All of them were his secret enemies, though they liked each other little more than they liked him. Even after Cortes finally reached Honduras (where he found Olid already overthrown, rendering the whole dolorous trek unnecessary), he did not communicate with Mexico for all the rest of the year 1525. By the end of that year his four governors, in intervals of fighting among themselves, had sent off to Cuba the only honest judge in Mexico with enough authority to challenge them; had tortured and executed Cortes' relative and personal agent Rodrigo de Paz, in trying to get Cortes' supposed hoard of gold; had demanded that everyone in the capital accept as a fact the death of Cortes and all his men, flogging the wife of Cortes' secretary Valiente (who was with him) with a hundred lashes for publicly doubting that her husband was dead; and finally co-Governor Salazar, the worst of the lot, had dragged Rodrigo de Paz's brother Pedro, the conquistador Andres de Tapia, and a number of others out of the sanctuary of the Franciscan house in Mexico City where they had placed themselves under the protection of the Church of Christ.

Mexico did not yet have a bishop, and very few priests except the Franciscans. Fray Martin of Valencia embodied almost all the ecclesiastical authority there was in New Spain. His authority extended only over his own churches; but there were almost no others, and he did not hesitate to use it. Turning away for a moment–we may imagine how reluctantly–from his deeply rewarding work of evangelizing the Indians, he laid Mexico City under an interdict, closing every Franciscan church there and removing the Blessed Sacrament from them. The tabernacle doors stood open; the priests were gone. Co-Governor Salazar may have feared neither God nor man, but he feared the Church militant. He backed down and released his prisoners.

News of the chaos in Mexico came to Emperor Charles in Spain. He sent Luis Ponce de Leon to take over its government if Cortes was in fact dead, and to conduct a thorough judicial investigation–called in Spanish law a *residencia*–if he were alive. Cortes and Ponce arrived in Mexico at almost the same moment, in the late spring of 1526; Cortes went at once to the Franciscan monastery in Mexico City for a six-day retreat, "giving account of my sins to God," as he wrote to Emperor Charles.[109] As soon as Ponce arrived, he and Cortes went to Mass together at the monastery. The next day Ponce presented his royal credentials; about ten days later, on July 20, 1526, he died–not uncommon for

Spaniards just arrived in a totally new environment, with strange food and drink, after a long and exhausting voyage.

This left Cortes' legal status in limbo for some time. Ponce had designated an elderly, infirm lawyer named Marcos de Aguilar as his successor; he too died in a few months and before his death named the devious former co-Governor Estrada as his successor. No *residencia* was held, but every sort of accusation and innuendo against Cortes was bandied about. The vicious Nuno de Guzman was named governor of Rio Panuco province north of Veracruz and immediately struck up a flourishing trade there in Indian slaves. Indians of that region down to six years of age were seized, branded in the face, and shipped off to the West Indies for a short life of hard labor. One of Cortes' men, named Cortijo, fought a duel with one for Estrada's officials, whereupon Estrada had Cortijo's hand cut off. Cortes decided, with good reason, that he could only end this anarchy by going to Spain himself and there seeking to regain the favor of Emperor Charles.

It was now the fall of 1527. The Franciscans had been preaching in Mexico for three years and had already made tens of thousand of converts. They had built a larger house in Mexico City, named San Francisco for their founder, with a famous high cross which could be seen from a great distance. The Mexican church even had its first martyr. He was from Tlaxcala, where the initial evangelization had been the most successful: the son of Chief Axotecatl, baptized Cristobal, killed by his father when Axotecatl rejected the new faith he had at first pretended to accept, while his son would not abandon it even to save his life.

Christianity was in Mexico to stay. But its advance was unquestionably slowed by the bad example many of the Spaniards were now giving, while the physical and linguistic obstacles remained enormous. Moreover, many Indians had the impression that the new faith was something alien, something belonging to white men which could only be mediated through them. It is a danger that confronts all missionary work, and especially in a situation such as this was, where the differences between cultures were so sharp, the contact had been so sudden, and the break with the past so complete.

The Indians waited, and watched. What did Christianity really mean to their conquerors? What did it really mean to them?

9.
Protector of the Indians
(1527-1531)

The decline and periodic breakdown of law and order in Mexico from the time of Cortes' departure for Honduras placed the Indians in even greater danger than the Spaniards. For Spaniards had rights under the law of Spain (it is an absurd myth of the "black legend" that theirs was a totalitarian society without legal guarantees for individual citizens); if those rights were not immediately enforced or protected because of the troubles, in time they would be vindicated, for Spaniards of that age were as tenacious in law as in battle. It was not uncommon to find courts adjudicating wrongs forty years old. But the Indians did not yet have clearly defined rights; the Crown and its legal authorities were still grappling with the manifold complexities of the situation in the New World as they groped their way toward legal definitions. Meanwhile the more brutal and greedy of the colonists were quick to take advantage of the uncertainty, particularly where it applied to forced labor.

In a society without beasts of burden, which had never even invented the wheel, almost all work and production depended directly on human labor. Finding the custom and practice of forced labor already in existence on a wide scale in Mexico, the conquistadors seized upon it eagerly for the production of food from their lands and to amass wealth for them. It was considered ignoble for a conquistador to farm or make goods himself. Mining was the hardest, most dangerous kind of labor, yet essential for the prosperity of the colony and to meet the immense financial needs of Emperor Charles V as he sought to discharge his duties as Holy Roman Emperor at a time when both infidels without (the Turks) and heretics within (the Protestants) were simultaneously on the attack. The conquerors were in full control of Mexico after one of the most spectacular and complete military victories in history. The King-Emperor was three thousand miles away across the ocean, usually a three months' voyage. The only practical restraint on the indiscriminate use of forced labor, up to and including death at hard labor in the mines, was the firm and strong authority of an honest, morally sensitive, respected and generally recognized royal governor. Mexico had had nothing like that since Cortes left for Honduras. Nor was even his moral authority always at a high level. He had burned four hundred rebels at the stake on the Rio Panuco, and had done some slave branding and trading himself, though only to prisoners taken in war against the Spaniards. All these problems suddenly came to a head at the court of Charles V, then being held at Burgos in Old Castile, in December of 1527. Cortes' letter of September 3 arrived, asking permission to come to Spain; with it, perhaps as its bearer, came sunny Alvarado, of whom Charles had heard much, whom he knew to be a close and trusted friend of Cortes. Alvardo was summoned at once to court where his full report did much to allay anti-Cortes sentiment. Mexico needed a government at once; for all practical purposes it now had none. Cortes could not provide it, for he was on his way to Spain. If he were vindicated, he might return as its governor. A stop–gap administration was needed, yet one which could make some investigation on the spot of the charges against Cortes, since the *residencia* which Ponce was supposed to have conducted had never been held due to his sudden death. As for the Church, both its rapid growth among the Indians and the troubles among the Spaniards showed the need for strong ecclesiastical authority to be established in Mexico. There was one bishop in the country now, Julian Garces, but he was a septuagenarian, rather inactive prelate who had no interest in the Indians. It was time to appoint a Bishop of Mexico City.

Charles acted with uncharacteristic haste. He made, at almost the same time, one of the finest appointments of his reign, and one of the worst.

On December 12, 1527, he nominated the Franciscan Juan de Zumarraga as bishop of Mexico City, with instructions to go to Mexico immediately as Bishop-Elect without waiting for confirmation by the Pope or episcopal consecration. Charles V had met Zumarraga for the first time in Holy Week that year, which the Emperor spent at the monastery of Abrojo near Valladolid where Zumarraga was prior. Impressed by the holy friar and his establishment, Charles had left a substantial gift. Zumarraga had not kept a peso, but distributed all of it among the poor.

This was the kind of bishop gold-hungry Mexico needed. In addition to his episcopal appointment, which Charles could only recommend until the Pope acted, Charles gave Zumarraga a public office with strong religious overtones: Protector of the Indians of Mexico. His instructions, dated January 10, 1528, declared:

> We order and charge and command you that you exercise solicitude in looking after and visiting said Indians, and see to it that they be well treated and taught in matters of our holy Catholic faith by those who are or will be in charge of them, and to study the laws and ordinances and instructions and provisions that have been given or shall be given concerning the kind treatment and conversion of said Indians.

And if any person or persons neglect to keep them [that is, the instructions concerning the kind treatment of the natives], you shall inflict on their persons and property the punishments contained therein, for which end, and for all the above-said in this letter, we give you full powers.[110]

Emperor Charles V had appointed a hero of the Faith–a man to whom the Mother of God would send a message, authenticated by her own portrait.

By contrast, at the very same time, Charles appointed a commission, or Audiencia, to govern Mexico, of which at least two of the four regular members (*oidores,* or Auditors) were unmitigated scoundrels; and a short time later, in April 1528, he appointed Nuno de Guzman president of the Audiencia and therefore, in effect, both governor of Mexico and conductor of the investigation of Cortes. Nuno de Guzman had been prominent at court during the early years of Charles' reign and had been closely associated with Charles' secretary, Francisco de los Cobos. The evils of Guzman's slave trading in the Rio Panuco region, of which he had been governor less than a year when he was appointed president of the Audiencia, were apparently then unknown in Spain. Still it was an extraordinary appointment. Donald Chipman, author of the only extended study of Guzman in English, who attempts the almost impossible task of improving Guzman's reputation, confesses himself "somewhat at a loss to explain why Nuno de Guzman received the appointment as president."[111] This appointment was a great and deadly error which was to bear heavily on all Mexico and nearly bring its evangelization to a halt.

To compound the irony, Bishop Zumarraga voyaged to Mexico on the same ship that carried his later violent enemies of the Audiencia. Cortes probably arrived at court just before they left. During the ensuring year he regained much, but not all, of Emperor Charles' favor. It would seem that, in the Emperor's judgment, Cortes' abandonment of his colony for the Honduras expedition constituted a decisive argument against ever entrusting him again with full authority for New Spain. Such a verdict may have been somewhat harsh, but under the circumstances it was not totally unjustified.

Bishop Zumarraga and the Auditors arrived at Veracruz in December 1528. The voyage had been very arduous; Zumarraga, who was nearly sixty years old, was sick for a month, and two of the four Auditors died. (Zumarraga had evidently come to know them all well during their long weeks on shipboard, for he later sadly remarked that God had allowed Mexico to be much afflicted by taking the wrong two!) Nuno de Guzman came down from the Rio Panuco to take control of Mexico on the first day of the New Year 1529. Before the month of January was over he and the two surviving Auditors of the Audiencia, Delgadillo and Matienzo, now hand in glove with him, had told Bishop Zumarraga not to press Indian complaints upon them nor to expect to exercise any real authority in his office as Protector of the Indians, for they would regard this as an infringement of their own authority. With patronizing contempt, he was told to stick to teaching his catechism–as though pagans could be converted by Christians who regarded that catechism as wholly irrelevant to the way they lived and governed.

It soon became very clear why Guzman and his two Auditor confederates did not want the office of Protector of the Indians to have any power. During the first eight months of 1529 they issued the appalling total of fifteen hundred slaving licenses, some for continuation of the traffic in Indians from Panuco, but more for shipping Indian slaves out of the three principal Gulf ports of Mexico: Veracruz, Coatzacoalcos, and the Rio de Grijalba. By September 1529 Bishop Zumarraga estimated that at least ten thousand Indians had been shipped from Mexico to the West Indies under authority given by Guzman, to be sold there as slaves with no prospect of ever returning to their homeland or to their families.

Nor was this all. Guzman and the Auditors shamelessly extorted gold and rich presents from the wealthier Indians and conscripted some ten thousand of the poorer ones to labor for their personal comfort, enjoyment, enrichment, and display, while allowing the infamous Salazar and other criminal officials a free hand to conduct extortions of their own. Auditor Delgadillo even stooped to raiding the Franciscan house at Texcoco, one of the first established by the twelve poor men, to carry off two Indian girls resident there whose beauty had caught his eye.

When Bishop Zumarraga protested against all this, the Audiencia summarily ordered him to stay out of all such matters and keep quiet about them. He consoled the suffering Indians as best he could, promising them that ultimately Emperor Charles would protect them and see that justice was done. (As the history of the next quarter-century was to show, that was no empty promise; but it must have been hard for the Indians to believe at the time.) Before long he said the same in a public declaration from the pulpit, whereupon the Audiencia, now drunk with irresponsible power, decreed the death penalty for any Indian appealing to the Bishop for help, and fines and imprisonment for any Spaniard who appealed to him.

Nevertheless the appeals continued, secretly and often at night. The Indians of Huejotzingo (where there was another of the houses originally established by Fray Martin's twelve Franciscans) told him that, in addition to their regular levy of labor under the *encomienda* system which was established throughout much of Mexico, they were required to supply (without pay) specified produce each day for the Auditors and also for their interpreter, Garcia del Pilar. When Zumarraga asked about this, Guzman threatened to hang him; and when Guzman learned the source of the complaint, he sent orders for the arrest of the Indians of Huejotzingo who were taking refuge in the Franciscan house. Zumarraga went there at once, and he and Motolinea, the prior of the house, protested vigorously but vainly as the Indians were dragged away. The Franciscans held a chapter meeting at Huejotzingo. Their current guardian, Luis de Fuensalida, who had succeeded Martin of Valencia when his three-year term ended in 1527, actually proposed that all the Franciscans in Mexico return to Spain, on the grounds that it was impossible to work under such a regime.

But when it came to a decision, the Franciscans would no more call retreat than Cortes after the Night of Sorrow. Fuensalida's proposal was voted down. The friars resolved to stay at whatever risk, and to denounce the Audiencia from the pulpit of the cathedral at pontifical high Mass on Pentecost Sunday, May 23, 1529. Fray Antonio Ortiz was given this dangerous assignment. He had hardly begun to speak when partisans of Salazar, on orders of Auditor Delgadillo, elbowed their way to the pulpit and pulled him down from it. When Bishop Zumarraga's chancellor invoked the automatic excommunication incurred by such behavior, the Auditors ordered him exiled from New Spain. Zumarraga patched up a temporary truce by giving those involved a mild penance (reciting the *Miserere*) which they performed, removing the excommunication, and they agreed to burn a libel they had recently circulated against the Franciscans.

It now began to dawn on Guzman and the Auditors that they had to deal, in Bishop Zumarraga and the Franciscan friars, with men of indomitable resolution ready, if necessary, to die for their Indians; and despite all their threats, they did not really dare to kill any of them. Furthermore, they could hardly fail to realize that in the discharge of their office they had gone far beyond anything that could possibly be defended or justified in the face of even the most rudimentary investigation. So they made every effort to block the transmission of any letter or message from the Franciscans to Spain. Several letters from Franciscan friars were intercepted at the coast. Meanwhile Bishop Zumarraga was engaged in drawing up a full report to Emperor Charles on the crimes and atrocities of the Guzman regime, including a detailed indictment of Guzman's slaving activities. It was ready by August 27–obviously just the kind of document the governor most wanted to intercept. How was the Bishop to get it out of Mexico? No one had any good idea. He decided to go to Veracruz himself to see how it might be done.

Bishop Zumarraga was a Basque, one of that race in the north of Spain speaking the strangest language in Europe, known since the earliest days of the Reconquest for its fervent Catholicism, which in these very years produced St. Ignatius of Loyola and St. Francis Xavier. Basques were also among the world's best seamen; it had been a Basque, Sebastian del Cano, who completed in 1522 the epochal voyage of Magellan around the world after his commander was killed in the Philippines, bringing home the only one of Magellan's ships that survived. Bishop Zumarraga found a fellow Basque on the waterfront in Veracruz, a sailor, who agreed to help him. (It is worthwhile to try to imagine the scene: the careworn but indefatigable bishop with his dark, commanding eyes, his brown Franciscan habit, his gentleness with a vein of iron, his episcopal dignity never standing in the way of communication with the humblest man or woman, his staggering responsibility for twenty million souls; and the sailor, barefoot, bearded, perhaps with a red sash about his waist, probably a man of passions and many sins, but touched by the closeness of this holy man, proud and honored that he was of his people and that the Bishop was asking for his help. Undoubtedly they carried on their discussion in Basque, confident that no one else within earshot was likely to be able to understand them.) The sailor had an idea, he would take the Bishop's letter and put it inside a slab of bacon, which in turn would be hidden in a barrel of oil. What arrangements were made to get the letter out of the oil and the bacon, once it reached Spain, we do not know. It would seem that the arrival of a report from the Bishop of Mexico City and the Protector of the Indians in Mexico in such a manner would speak more loudly even than the damning words it contained, about conditions in Mexico.

In fact, some knowledge of these conditions was already coming to Spain. In the absence of Emperor Charles in Italy, his wife, Empress Isabel, had already issued a blistering order to exile from the New World anyone who interfered with the transmission of personal correspondence from there to Spain.

The first reports of the favors being granted to Cortes by Emperor Charles had begun to reach Mexico in August. In a fit of anger at the news, Salazar cried out in public: "A king who sends us such a traitor as Cortes is a heretic and no Christian!"[112] Alvarado, who was in Mexico City at the time, charged Salazar formally to the Audiencia with incitement to rebellion. Guzman's response was to put Alvarado in chains.

It could not go on. Guzman, much the most intelligent of the tyrants of the First Audiencia, decided to leave the two Auditors sunk in their luxury and lechery as the day of reckoning approached, while he undertook a glittering new conquest which would cause the past, at least in his case, to be forgotten. On December 22, 1529 he set out for the west with a force of 200 cavalry, 300 Spanish infantry and 10,000 Indian allies to conquer the lands between the Valley of Mexico and the Pacific Ocean, beginning with the kingdom of Michoacan to the southwest which had been the nearest major civilized region not incorporated into the Aztec empire. In these lands no royal commissions ran, and Bishop Zumarraga had no authority. They would be his, he was confident, if he could conquer them. During the whole of the year 1530 Nuno de Guzman cut a swath of terror through the Mexican west. He tortured and then executed the king of Michoacan, trying to get more gold; he burned Cuinao, the capital of the next province westward; he reached the Pacific in May; and by the fall he had a new slaving operation underway. During the next several years, some five thousand Indians of Jalisco (the province around the present city of Guadalajara) were seized, branded in the face, and shipped to the Rio Panuco under Guzman's authority for slave labor there or for transshipment to the West Indies.

Meanwhile in Mexico, after the kidnapping and torture of two priests who had been partisans of Cortes and were taken from the sanctuary of the monastery of San Francisco in Mexico City, Bishop Zumarraga laid the city under an interdict and formally excommunicated Auditors Delgadillo and Matienzo. This was no excommunication that could be removed by reciting the *Miserere*. He lifted the interdict at Easter of 1530, but kept the excommunication in effect, since the auditors not only would not yield, but executed one of the two priests and flogged and maimed the other.

In Spain Bishop Zumarraga's letter of August 27, 1529, smuggled out in the bacon slab in the oil barrel, had produced its anticipated effect. By March 1530 Empress Isabel had decided to appoint a new Audiencia, headed by Bishop Sebastian Ramirez de Fuenleal, a man of universally recognized probity and ability, currently president of the Audiencia and Bishop of Santo Domingo. Selection of the Auditors was entrusted to the aged and holy Bishop of Badajoz, who picked four men as different as could be imagined from Delgadillo and Matienzo. One of them was Vasco de Quiroga, at that time a layman, later to be ordained and consecrated Bishop of Michoacan, its chief evangelizer and great benefactor, still remembered and revered by its people as "Tata Vasco" (Grandpa Vasco), who overlaid the evil that Guzman had done in his conquest of Michoacan, by the superlative good of half a lifetime devoted to the service of its Indian people.

In August 1530 a royal decree, issued in the name of Emperor Charles V, finally prohibited the enslavement of the Indians.

No person shall dare to make a single Indian a slave whether in war or in peace . . . whether by barter, by purchase, by trade, or on any other pretext or cause whatever.[113]

The decree also confirmed Bishop Zumarraga as Protector of the Indians and more precisely defined his legal powers. Later that month the Auditors of the new Audiencia sailed from Seville. (Cortes had already returned, with the title of Captain-General–but not governor–and Marquis of the Valley of Oaxaca.) They arrived around the end of the year and took over the government on January 9, 1531, though Bishop Fuenleal did not arrive until September. A *residencia* was immediately proclaimed for the First Audiencia. As the complaints against them poured in, Guzman's property in the Rio Panuco region was sequestered, and Delgadillo and Matienzo were arrested.

But it was not yet the full day of reckoning for Nuno de Guzman. Just as he had calculated, he was given the initial governorship of the region he had discovered and conquered (the usual practice with conquistadors), which he called New Galicia. His misrule there was allowed to continue for five more years before another *residencia* at last brought him to justice.

10.
The Portrait of the Mother of God
(December 1531)

It had now been twelve years since the landing of Cortes, and ten since the fall of the Hummingbird Wizard. A stratified colonial society was already beginning to develop in Mexico, with the conquistadors and those who had come in their train the privileged class, and the Indians below them regarded primarily as servants. This was not what Cortes or any of the best of the Spaniards had intended. Their goal had been a united Christian community, truly a new Spain. The cultural amalgamation required would have taken a long time in any case, and was now sure to be strongly resented by those who preferred the master-servant relationship. But the conversion of the Indians was the indispensable starting point, and this was retarded by their sheer numbers and the very small number of active missionaries, and by the resentments and suspicions naturally generated among the Indians by the manner in which such men as Salazar, Delgadillo, Matienzo and Guzman had exercised their power, even if only for relatively short periods of time.

No Indian living in Mexico had ever seen Emperor Charles V; he was never likely to come there, nor were the few Indians who were sent to Spain likely to return. They did not really understand who Emperor Charles was, the unique office he held as both King of Spain and temporal head of Christendom. They had no particular reason to trust him. There is overwhelming evidence of their trust in, and even love for Cortes (whom they still called "Malinche"), but the manner in which he had been treated by the Spanish authorities, even if there might be some good reasons for it, was hardly likely to promote confidence in those authorities among the Indians.

Furthermore, it must never be forgotten how their world had been shattered. It had been a fantastically evil world; but that was not the fault of the *macehualtin*, the Indian poor; they had been its victims, not its creators. It was all they had known. Liberated from its evil, they were left floating–no longer Aztecs, but not Spaniards either. They needed a whole new ground for their lives. If that ground were to be Christianity, as Fray Martin of Valencia and Fray Toribio Motolinea and Bishop Zumarraga and their companions so ardently desired, it must become part of *them– their* faith, not only or primarily the faith of their conquerors.

This was the need of the Indians. As for the Spaniards, those who were beginning to forget needed to be reminded that the real crushers of Satan are not fallen men, but the perfect God and His sinless Mother, and that they care for all men equally without distinction of race or culture. In a word, it was time for Juan Diego to receive his visit.

Few lives have spanned such awesome changes as his. Growing up on the shore of Lake Texcoco, thirteen years old at the time of Tlacaellel's sacrifice of the eighty thousand, dwelling there all through Cortes' first arrival, the Night of Sorrow, the Battle of Otumba (Cortes on his march to Otumba must have passed within a few miles of Juan Diego's hut), the return from Tlaxcala, and the final triumph in Mexico City; becoming a Christian in 1525 and being baptized Juan Diego, along with his faithful, gentle wife who was baptized Maria Lucia, and his uncle who was baptized Juan Bernardino; beholding the chaos of the time of the four governors and the explosions of hatred, lust, and fear that marked the time of the First Audiencia of Guzman, Juan Diego had seen some of the most extraordinary history of all ages unfold before his eyes. He was now fifty-seven years old; but all of it had left him still simple, kind, loving, childlike in mind and heart. It seems he must always have been a person like this; his conversion and his baptism would have made him more so.

We have the account of what happend in December 1531 on the hill of Tepeyac overlooking Lake Texcoco and Mexico City from Antonio Valeriano, one of the finest Indian scholars at the College of Santiago de Tlatelolco, set up by the Franciscans in 1536 for the higher education of the Indians in the suburb of Mexico City nearest Tepeyac, proficient in Latin, Spanish, and Nahuatl. Valeriano knew Juan Diego personally and, by all indications, wrote his account of the apparitions before Juan Diego died in 1548, on the basis of Juan Diego's direct testimony. This document, in Nahuatl, is known as the *Nican Mopohua* from its first two words. What is either the original or a very early copy, almost contemporary with the original, was recently rediscovered by Jesuit Father Ernest J. Burrus in the New York Public Library. It should lay to rest once and for all the claim that there is no adequate contemporary historical record of the apparitions of Our Lady of Guadalupe.[114]

At dawn Saturday, December 9, 1531, the day after the feast of the Immaculate Conception, Juan Diego was on his way from the village of Tolpetlac near Cuauhtitlan, where he now lived, to Tlatelolco for morning Mass, which he attended every day when he possibly could. His route ran over the hill of Tepeyac and across the Tepeyac causeway to Tlatelolco next to Mexico City, where Gonzalo de Sandoval had fought his way during the great siege ten years earlier. As Juan Diego came to the summit of the hill he heard singing, and saw a brilliant white cloud aureoled in rainbow. The white light was coming from the midst of the cloud, and was intensely bright. A beautiful young woman appeared before the cloud, her clothes shining so gloriously that they seemed to turn rocks into pendants of jewels, cactus leaves into emeralds, cactus trunks into gold. (When the

Blessed Virgin Mary first appeared at Fatima in Portugal 386 years later, in May 1917, Lucia saw her clad in a white which she described as "more brilliant than the sun dispensing light, clearer and more intense than a crystal cup full of crystalline water penetrated by the rays of the most glaring sun."[115]

Juan Diego fell to his knees. The lady said, speaking in his own Nahuatl language: "My son, Juan Diego, where are you going?" "Noble lady," he answered, "I am on my way to the church at Tlatelolco to hear Mass."[116] Then she said:

> You must know and be very certain in your heart, my son, that I am truly the perpetual and perfect Virgin Mary, holy mother of the True God through whom everything lives, the Creator and Master of Heaven and Earth.
>
> I wish and intensely desire that in this place my sanctuary be erected so that in it I may show and make known and give all my love, my compassion, my help and my protection to the people. I am your merciful mother, the mother of all of you who live united in this land, and of all mankind, of all those who love me, of those who cry to me, of those who seek me, of those who have confidence in me. Here I will hear their weeping, their sorrow, and will remedy and alleviate their suffering, necessities and misfortunes.
>
> And so that my intentions may be known, you must go to the house of the bishop of Mexico and tell him that I sent you and that it is my desire to have a sanctuary built here.[117]

Mary had come to claim the conquest Hernan Cortes had made in her name. She had come to call upon all now dwelling in Mexico to "live united in this land" and to ask her to help them in their need, raising the shining shield of her eternal love over a people who had been victimized more than any other on earth.

Juan Diego hastened to do her bidding and spoke to Bishop Zumarraga. Not surprisingly, he doubted and told the unknown Indian to come again later at a more convenient time. Juan Diego returned to the hill of Tepeyac about sunset. The lady of light was waiting just as he had seen her at dawn. He urged her to send someone to the Bishop more distinguished and so more likely to be believed.

> I am only a poor man. I am not worthy of being there where you send me. Pardon me, my Queen, I do not want to make your noble heart sad, I do not want to fall into your displeasure.[118]

But Mary told him that it was he, and no other, that she wished to send, that he should carry her message to Bishop Zumarraga again on the following day. He left her, calling her "my Dear One, my Lady."[119]

The next day, December 10, was Sunday, Mass was later in the morning. After it was over, Juan Diego went again to the Bishop's house and, after much difficulty with the guards, gained admittance. The Bishop questioned him, more impressed this time. But he told him that the lady must provide some proof that she really was the Mother of God. Then he sent two of his attendants to follow Juan Diego, but they lost his track.

At sunset of this day Juan Diego was back on the hill of Tepeyac again, where the Lady was waiting for him and assured him that the next day she would give him the sign the Bishop had asked for. But when he reached home that evening he found his uncle Juan Bernardino very ill. All day Monday, December 11 he cared for his uncle, rather than returning to Bishop Zumarraga or to Tepeyac. Juan Bernardino thought that he was going to die and asked his nephew to go to Tlatelolco to bring back a priest to anoint him. On Tuesday morning, December 12, Juan Diego started out, avoiding the top of Tepeyac hill out of fear and embarrassment because he had not kept his promise to return there. But Mary came down the side of the hill to intercept him, asking him where he was going. He explained about his uncle. She responded:

> Listen and be sure, my dear son, that I will protect you; do not be frightened or grieve, or let your heart be dismayed, however great the illness may be that you speak of. Am I not here? I, who am your Mother, and is not my help a refuge? Am I not of your kind? Do not be concerned about your uncle's illness, for he is not going to die. Be assured, he is already well. Is there anything else that you need?[120]

"*Am I not of your kind?*" With these words, the Blessed Virgin Mary, the Mother of God, gave back to those who had been Satan's captives their dignity and their hope. She was of their kind. She was no alien, no stranger. She was theirs.

Then she told Juan Diego to climb up the hill, saying that he would find flowers blooming there which he should pluck and bring to her. The hill was a desert place where only cactus, thistles and thornbush grew. Juan Diego had never seen a flower there. But when he reached the top, it was covered with beautiful Castilian roses, touched with dew, of exquisite fragrance. Mary took them from him as he gathered them, arranged them with her own hands, and put them in his cloak, or *tilma*, made of the fiber of the maguey cactus, and tied a knot in it behind his neck to hold the roses in place. (We are vividly reminded, in visualizing this–as Juan Diego very likely was reminded as it happened–of a mother helping a little son into his fine clothes.) She told him:

> This is the sign that you must take to the Lord Bishop. In my name tell him that with this he will see and recognize my will and that he must do what I ask; and you who are my ambassador worthy of my confidence, I counsel you to take every care that you open your mouth only in the presence of the Bishop, and you must make it known to him what it is that you carry, and tell him how I asked you to climb to the top of the hill to gather the flowers. Tell him also all that you have seen, so that you will persuade the Lord Bishop and he will see that the church is built for which I ask.[121]

When he arrived again at the Bishop's house Juan Diego was kept waiting a long time by the Bishop's attendants, who eventually insisted on seeing the roses; but when they tried to take some of them they could not, because they became "not roses that they touched, but were as if painted or embroidered."[122] When they finally admitted him to the Bishop's presence, Juan Diego told him all that had happened, and opened his cloak. The roses cascaded to the floor; and there upon the *tilma* was a full portrait of the Mother of God, in Indian dress, her small hands joined in prayer, her soft black hair falling gently upon her shoulders under her cape and framing the perfect oval of her face, with half-closed eyes deep as the sea, and the rosebud mouth, slightly smiling, that had kissed the Infant God on Christmas Day in Bethlehem.

That portrait still exists today, just as it was then, in brilliant color, the normally short-lived cactus fiber cloth untouched by the passage of over 450 years. Anyone can go to Mexico City and see it.

Bishop Juan de Zumarraga fell to his knees. It had been given to him to see what even his supremely holy master, St. Francis of Assisi, had never seen in this life: the face and form of the Blessed Virgin Mary, her own portrait. The tears streamed down his worn cheeks as he prayed her forgiveness for having doubted her and her messenger. When he could speak and stand again, he reverently took the cloak from Juan Diego and brought it to his chapel to lay it before her Son present in the Blessed Sacrament.

Juan Diego remained with Bishop Zumarraga that night. We would give much to know what they talked about. But no word of Bishop Zumarraga's on this greatest event of his life has survived to our day. Nevertheless, we have explicit testimony that Archbishop Garcia de Mendoza in 1601 had in the archdiocesan archives of Mexico City a full and circumstantial account and judicial Acts of the apparition prepared by Bishop Zumarraga, which Dr. Alonso Munoz de la Torre once found him reading; while Fray Pedro de Mezquia states categorically that he read in the Franciscan monastery at Virotia in Spain in the eighteenth century an account of the apparitions by Zumarraga which he had sent back to Spain. Both these documents have unfortunately disappeared, but the evidence is solid that they once existed; and the *Nican Mopohua* is enough for full authentication since it was written while Bishop Zumarraga was still alive and in Mexico (he died the same year as Juan Diego, 1548) by Valeriano, who as the best Latin scholar of the college of Santiago de Tlatelolco undoubtedly knew the bishop personally and well.

But the best evidence that the Blessed Virgin Mary truly visited Juan Diego on the hill of Tepeyac must always be her portrait itself. Recently, in 1979, it underwent one of its most searching scientific studies, made by Dr. Philip Callahan, a research biophysicist at the University of Florida, who is also a painter, a photographer and a scientific writer. Photographing it extensively for the first time in infra-red light, a recommended technique for the critical study of old paintings, Dr. Callahan found evidence that some minor decorations on the portrait–the sunburst around Mary, the gold stars under the moon, whose paint is clearly cracking and fading– were added or painted over much later by human hands, probably after the great floods in Mexico City during the years 1629-1634 which did some damage to the *tilma* which bore the sacred image. (In confirmation, the sunburst does not appear in early representations of the sacred image in Indian picture-writing.) But regarding the rest of the portrait, including every aspect of Mary's own face and form, Dr. Callahan's conclusion was very different.

> The mantle is of dark turquoise blue. . . . This presents an inexplicable phenomenon because all such pigments are semi-permanent and known to be subject to considerable fading with time, especially in hot climates. The Indian Mayan blue wall paintings are already badly faded. The blue mantle, however, is bright enough to have been laid last week.[123] [It is this incredible brightness of the colors in the portrait that first impresses and astonishes nearly every visitor to the shrine of Our Lady of Guadalupe in Mexico City today.]

> The most notable feature of the robe is its remarkable luminosity. It is highly reflective of visible radiation yet transparent to the infrared rays. . . . As in the case of the blue mantle, the shadowing of the pink robe is blended under the pink pigment. . . .
> The pink pigment appears to be inexplicable. . . . One of the really strange aspects of this painting is that not only is the tilma not sized, but there is absolutely no protective coating of varnish. Despite this

unusual total lack of any protective overcoating, the robe and mantle are as bright and colored as if the paint were newly laid.[124]

The head of the Virgin of Guadalupe is one of the great masterpieces of artistic facial expressions. In subtleness of form, simplicity of execution, hue and coloring it has few equals among the masterpieces of the world. Furthermore, there are no portraits that I have ever observed which are executed in a similar manner. . . .

One of the truly marvelous and inexplicable techniques utilized to give realism to the painting is the way that it takes advantage of the unsized tilma to give it depth and render it lifelike. This is particularly evident in the mouth, where a coarse fiber of the fabric is raised above the level of the rest of the weave and follows perfectly the ridge at the top of the lip. The same rough imperfections occur below the highlighted area on the left cheek and to the right and below the right eye. I would consider it impossible that any human painter could select a tilma with imperfections of weave positioned so as to accentuate the shadows and highlights in order to impart realism. The possibility of coincidence is even more unlikely. . . . The black of the eyes and hair cannot be iron oxide or any pigment that turns brown with age for the paint is neither cracked nor faded with age. The truly phenomenal thing about the face and hands is the tonal quality which is as much a physical effect from light reflecting off the coarse tilma as it is from the paint itself. . . . At a distance, where the pigment and surface sculpturing blend together, the overwhelming beauty of the olive-colored Madonna emerges as if by magic. The expression suddenly appears reverent yet joyous, Indian yet European, olive-skinned yet white of hue.[125]

Furthermore, greatly enlarged photographs of the right eye of the Blessed Virgin Mary in the portrait have revealed three human figures, one of whom appears to be Juan Diego and another his interpreter when speaking to Bishop Zumarraga, Juan Gonzalez, who later became a zealous supporter of devotion to Our Lady of Guadalupe. We have portraits of both Juan Diego and Juan Gonzalez, showing a strong resemblance to two of these figures in the eye.[126]

News of the miracle spread rapidly through the Valley of Mexico. The day after the revelation of the portrait of the Blessed Virgin Mary, Bishop Zumarraga and Juan Diego went to Tepeyac accompanied by a large group. Juan Diego naturally wanted to hurry on to see his uncle, though he must have believed him cured since Mary had said he surely would be. Indeed, he was; and he told them that she had come to him also, as he lay helpless in his illness, naming herself to him as "Holy Mary of Guadalupe."

101

Guadalupe was, and is one of the most significant shrines to the Blessed Virgin Mary in Spain, but has no visible connection with the apparition in Mexico. There has been much speculation that Our Lady actually used some Nahuatl word (many suggestions have been made as to what word it might have been) which sounded to the Spanish like "Guadalupe," a very Spanish word that would be hard for Nahuatl speakers to pronounce, since their language has no "g" and no "d". All such speculation overlooks the fact that Juan Diego and his uncle were presenting their accounts of the apparitions to Bishop Zumarraga through a trained interpreter, Juan Gonzalez, whose native language was Nahuatl but who also spoke Spanish well, and therefore would have been most unlikely to have misheard or mistranslated some Nahuatl name or title as "Guadalupe." Therefore this must really have been the name she chose–perhaps as another way of showing how she wanted her children in Spain and in Mexico to draw closer together.

Juan Diego and his uncle returned to Bishop Zumarraga's house, where they and many others began to plan the quick erection of a simple shrine where she had requested it, on the side of Tepeyac hill. The most readily available construction material, which could be used much more quickly than any other to put up a building, was adobe–sun-dried clay. Many willing hands assisted in the task, and a small building was ready to house the glorious image on the indicated site in less than two weeks. It was completed just before Christmas. Bishop Zumarraga ordered its dedication with much rejoicing and a great procession on the second day of Christmas, December 26, 1531. He sent a special invitation to Cortes and his second wife, recently come from Spain, to attend the dedication and join in the procession. The letter of invitation, from Bishop Zumarraga to Cortes, was discovered some years ago in the immense and still not fully explored Archives of the Indies in Spain by the devoted researches of the great Mexican Church historian P. Mariano Cuevas, S.J. Though not entirely clear because of its allusions to prior correspondence or conversations between the two men, not now known, it is the nearest we have to a contemporary document attesting to the miracle:

> Illustrious and most fortunate lord! Give thanks to the Lord our God, resolving to serve him more fully henceforth. . . . Have patience tomorrow with the play we put on, it will give pleasure on the joyous Nativity of Our Savior and how splendid it will be! Before long I revealed it [Bishop Zumarraga does not say what he revealed; Father Cuevas thinks this refers to the circumstances of the apparition which at first he had been reluctant to discuss] and at sunset walked my stations of St. Francis first at the Great Church, and then those of

St. Dominic. The bishop of Tlaxcala preaches tomorrow. And now I am in charge of my procession and am writing to Veracruz. It is impossible to describe the joy of everyone. It is not necessary to write to [Cristobal de] Salamanca. I sent a messenger to the custodian [of the Franciscan house] at Cuernavaca. An Indian has already gone to Father Toribio [Motolinea]. All praise to God, and the dances of the Indians; all praise to the name of God on the eve of the fiesta of fiestas.

Say to her ladyship [Cortes' wife] that I wish to give the Great Church the name of the Conception of the Mother of God, since on that occasion God and His Mother willed to grant this favor to this land which you won.[127]

Father Cuevas points out that in the Sevillan missal which was then used in Mexico, the feast of the Immaculate Conception was not confined to the single day of December 8, but, like Christmas, extended over a number of days, from December 8 to 17. Thus the reference to the great favor from God "to this land which you won" happening on the occasion of the Immaculate Conception could refer to any event during this ten-day period, and would seem likely to refer to the apparitions which took place December 9, 10, and 12. Were it not for this reference to the special favor (*merced*) from God, the letter could be regarded as alluding simply to Christmas celebrations. The Guadalupan tradition, attested by several of the elderly witnesses at the formal investigation in Mexico City in 1666 who reported what they had heard of the miracle from their parents and grandparents recalls a great celebration at the first installation of the portrait in the original shrine on Tepeyac December 26, 1531. This tradition receives considerable confirmation from this letter of Bishop Zumarraga.

If this be the meaning of the letter, as seems probable, it is particularly noteworthy that the great bishop made a point of paying tribute to Hernan Cortes, in the direct context of Our Lady's gift of her own portrait, by speaking of Mexico, the land to which that splendid favor had been given, as the land that he had won. It suggests that Bishop Zumarraga believed, as we have proposed here, that the victory of the Catholic army of Cortes over the gods of darkness and death was necessary before the Blessed Virgin Mary could come to Mexico.

Indians and Spaniards came together to venerate the surpassingly beautiful image, children together of the Mother of all the faithful. They came on December 26, 1531, and they have been coming ever since–day and night, season after season, decade after decade, century after century. Later the Church was to proclaim Our Lady of Guadalupe the patroness of all the Americas, the whole great span from Arctic to Antarctic that the sailors and conquistadors of Catholic Spain revealed to the world.

103

11.
Nine Million Baptisms
(1531-1548)

The holy Fray Martin of Valencia, head of the Franciscan party of twelve missionaries who really began the evangelization of Mexico, wrote to Charles V in November 1532, less than a year after the apparition of Our Lady of Guadalupe, that up to then about 200,000 Indians had been baptized–a small fraction, probably little more than one percent, of the total population of the land. His letter probably arrived in Spain shortly before Bishop Zumarraga himself, who had been temporarily recalled there to give a personal report, and above all to receive his episcopal consecration. He was consecrated Bishop of Mexico in Valladolid in Castile, delivering a moving and powerful homily on the glory of spiritual warfare and triumph for the sake of Christ. When Bishop Zumarraga returned to Mexico in October 1534, he found that a tremendous outpouring of grace among the Indians of Mexico had begun, and was swelling into a tide.

Careful records were maintained by Father Toribio Motolinea, the poor man of Tlaxcala, who was already at work on his great history of the Indians of New Spain. Writing in 1536, he reports that he and one other priest had baptized 14,200 Indians in five days. In Mexico as a whole, he declared that there had been no less than five million baptisms since the arrival of the twelve under Fray Martin in 1524. Comparing this total with Fray Martin's 200,000 of 1532, it is clear that the vast majority of these baptisms took place in the four years from 1532 to 1536–a period when, as Robert Ricard states, "evangelization [in Mexico] made an immense jump, and it is certain that the average number of baptisms was much greater between 1532 and 1536 than between 1524 and 1532."[128] Wherever the missionaries were, wherever they went, Indians of all ages flocked to them for baptism in unprecedented, overwhelming numbers. These numbers necessitated omission of some elements of the usual baptismal liturgy, such as the rites of the salt and the saliva, and the use of consecrated oil (supplies of which were limited). But Motolinea is unequivocal that every candidate was individually baptized and every adult presenting himself for baptism was given two oral summaries of the catechism. Therefore instruction, though brief, was never lacking. Nor was any pressure, to say nothing of force, employed. On the contrary, it was the missionaries who were pressured and almost unbearably overburdened by the tide of converts, so much greater than they had prepared for or ever expected so soon. We hear of Indians coming to them for baptism when they approached villages for the first time, before their preaching had even begun.

The flood of baptisms continued during all the remaining years of the life of Juan Diego and of Bishop Zumarraga, who died within a few days of each other in the spring of 1548. By then the total number of baptized Indians in Mexico was approximately nine million.[129] The validity of the baptisms with an abbreviated liturgy performed during the period 1532-36 was confirmed in effect by the bull of Pope Paul III issued June 1, 1537, though the Pope directed that there be fewer omissions from the baptismal liturgy in the future.

In Tlaxcala in particular, Christian fervor reached great heights. Easter of 1536 was celebrated in Tlaxcala with thousands of special offerings by the Indians decorated with Christian symbols, and by a reverent dawn procession. The celebration of Corpus Christi of 1538 was still more full and memorable:

> The procession of the Most Holy Sacrament was accompanied by files of Indians bearing crosses and saints' images, worked in gold and feathers. Their route was decorated in the form of a three-aisled church, in which the Host and ministers occupied the center, and the congregation the outer aisles. Over a thousand floral arches simulated the form of an actual religious building. . . . Later, religious plays were given, representing the annunciation of the birth of John the Baptist and other events of Christian history.[130]

The young men of Tlaxcala who had been educated during these years in the Franciscan house went out with a burning enthusiasm to convert and teach their people and make the new faith far more than a matter of occasional rites, to make it the center of their lives. Many Indian girls, educated at convent schools, joined them, teaching Christian doctrine in the homes of the Indians and making more conversions. Jeronimo de Mendieta, who arrived in Mexico in 1554 and wrote his ecclesiastical history of the Indians from 1572 to 1596, entitles one of this chapters covering this period: "How the conversion of the Indians was done through children."[131]

Though most conventional historians of Mexico today prefer not to mention Our Lady of Guadalupe (or at least, not at the point in time when she appeared), it should be self-evident that this immense surge of baptisms beginning in 1532–these millions of Indians suddenly seeking out the sacrament of Christian initiation with an overwhelming desire, even when not yet in contact with the missionaries, where most of them had previously held back despite the best efforts of the missionaries and the prestige of the conquerors–derived primarily from the impact of the apparition and the portrait, once news of them had spread throughout the land during the course of the year 1532. The Franciscans at this time recognized and honored Our Lady of Guadalupe; they organized a procession to her shrine to pray for relief from an epidemic in 1544. The public criticism of the devotion to Our Lady of Guadalupe some years later, in 1566, by the then Franciscan provincial in Mexico, Fray Francisco de Bustamante–of which so much has been made by critics of the historicity of the apparition and the spiritual significance of the devotion–represented only his personal opinion, and probably that of some other Franciscans at that time; but the Archbishop of Mexico in 1556, Alonso de Montufar, Zumarraga's successor, was and remained an ardent advocate and defender of Our Lady of Guadalupe.

Juan Diego, who devoted the rest of his life to the constant care of the little sanctuary where the sacred image was kept, became famed among the Indians for his sanctity, and is represented in their contemporary picture-writing with the signs of a holy man.[132] Gabriel Saurez, an Indian, testified at the formal hearing of 1666 at the age of 110 that his father, Mateo Saurez, had known Juan Diego well, had seen the sacred image while Juan Diego was still living, "and knew many who had gone to the hermitage to ask Juan Diego to pray for them."[133] Another witness at the 1666 hearings, Pablo Juarez, chief of Cuauhtitlan, whose grandmother had been a close friend of Juan Diego who had grown up in that town, said that the apparition of Our Lady of Guadalupe was "matter so public and well-known, how it happened, that even the children sang all about it in their games."[134] And we have the will of Juana Martin of Cuauhtitlan, a relative of Juan Diego, a nearly contemporary document dated March 11, 1559, which mentions Juan Diego and declares that:

> Through him, the miracle took place over there in Tepeyac, where the beloved Lady Holy Mary appeared, whose lovely image we see in Guadalupe, which is really ours and of our town of Cuauhtitlan. And now, with all my heart. my soul and my will, I give to Her Majesty all that is really mine. . . . I give it all to the Virgin of Tepeyac.[135]

To regard the "immense jump" in baptisms and the desire of the Indians for conversion that began in 1532, and the well attested appearance of the Blessed Virgin Mary and her portrait in December 1531, as a mere coincidence, passes all bounds of rational probability. There had to be a connection; and assuredly, there was.

106

The result of the nine million baptisms by the time of the death of Juan Diego and Bishop Zumarraga in 1548 was the creation of large Christian Indian communities throughout most of central Mexico, where a substantial majority of the population was now Christian. They were usually separate from the Spanish communities, with great church-monastery complexes around which the Indian dwellings were gathered. The churches were decorated by Indian artists with frescoes and sculptures a universe removed from the horrors they had painted and carved in the days of the Hummingbird Wizard. The liturgy was celebrated with music played and sometimes composed by the Indians, and dramatized by Nahuatl plays (the earliest known, written by the Franciscan Fray Luis de Fuensalida probably before 1535, is of the Annunciation). The numbers of the new Indian Catholic communities were limited only by the number of the missionaries and of their Indian assistants who could be trusted to lead such communities in the absence of a Spanish priest or lay brother.

It is not at all surprising that in later years it was found that some of these new converts had later secretly apostatized, and that the old religion was not entirely dead. That could have been expected. The truly significant fact is the vast extent, the general depth, and above all the historical endurance of the conversion. In the fifteen years after the appearance of Our Lady of Guadalupe on Tepeyac hill, the nine million baptisms she inspired created Catholic Mexico–Indian as much as Spanish, devoted, indestructible, surviving devastating epidemics and long-continued economic oppression and even the terrible mistake of the Spanish Church and the governmental authorities in later deciding (after Bishop Zumarraga's death) not to ordain native priests. In more recent times Catholic Mexico has survived revolutions and bitterly anti-Catholic governments, ever continuing to draw strength and grace from the inexhaustible foundation of both whose gentle face has glowed undimmed for more than four hundred and fifty years on Juan Diego's *tilma*.

12.
"Am I Not Here?"

The Blessed Virgin Mary, Mother of God, Mother of Sorrows, does not come to take away the Cross of Christ, but rather to give it.

She came to Lourdes in 1857 to heal the sick, and since then she has healed there thousands whose cures scientific medicine cannot explain; but the majority who come to Lourdes are not healed, but go back to home or hospital to bear their cross anew, to suffer and die. She came to Fatima in 1917 during the First World War in response to Pope Benedict XV's anguished prayers for peace, for an end to the horrible and pointless slaughter of that war; she asked more prayers for peace, and finally announced that peace would come–only to be followed by another, still greater war and by the advance of a great evil out of Russia to spread all over the world. When she came to Tepeyac in 1531 after the conquest of Mexico, she brought about the conversion of its people; but that conversion has been followed by much oppression and persecution.

The story of that oppression and persecution in Mexico–oppression by many of the wealthy and powerful among the descendants of the First Spanish settlers, and persecution by the anti-Catholic governments that have dominated Mexico most of the time since 1832–has often been told, perhaps too often. What has hardly been told at all is the far more important story of the preservation of the Faith in Mexico despite it all. There has never been a major anti-Catholic movement among the ordinary people of Mexico; virtually all of the hostility to the Faith has come from a small elitist minority. This fact becomes much more remarkable when it is realized that for three hundred years the Mexican Church had no priests of its own; all of its priests were Spanish, and with the passage of time from the heroic missionary era of the sixteenth century, many of these Spanish priests became far removed in spirit, and sometimes in body, from the people they were intended to serve. There were always noble exceptions, but not nearly enough to account for the unwavering constancy of faith in Catholic Mexico.

The Virgin of Guadalupe accounts for it. She had said to Juan Diego:

> Listen and be sure, my dear son, that I will protect you; do not be frightened or grieve, or let your heart be dismayed. . . . Am I not here? I, who am your Mother, and is not my help a refuge? Am I not of your kind?[136]

Against every oppressor, against every persecutor, her figure stood: *Maria Morena*, the dark Virgin, gentle, loving, invulnerable, inextinguishably shining. Neither narrow-minded later Spaniards who disapproved of her too common associations (there has always been a certain type of Christian who tends to find Mary very undignified) nor anti-Catholic fanatics who saw the Church as the supreme obstacle to what they called "progress," dared for centuries to touch her. But they could not forget that she was there. Finally, in perhaps the greatest crisis in Mexican history after the conquest itself, when the revolutionary constitution of 1917 (the year Mary appeared at Fatima) had turned over full control of the Church of Mexico to the bitterly anti-Catholic government of Obregon and Calles, the Church's enemies struck at Our Lady of Guadalupe directly. A bomb was concealed in a bouquet of flowers placed under her sacred image on November 14, 1921. It exploded during Mass. Pieces of stone were ripped from the sanctuary; the force of the explosion twisted a heavy metal cross on the altar into an almost circular shape. But not one worshipper in the packed church was hurt; and the sacred image was absolutely untouched.

A chapel of reparation was later added to the church of Our Lady of Guadalupe, with the twisted cross placed in it to remind the faithful of the evil that had struck and the protection that had been given. The symbolism was also profound. For it is the Cross that good Christians must bear, the Cross that represents both the power of the forces of destruction and the means of redemption; but the Mother of God is forever safe, and her portrait belongs to the Catholic people of Mexico and will not be taken from them.

Mexico's faith survived Obregon and Calles, as it had survived all its enemies before them, aided by the crusading heroes known as the *cristeros* who fought them in the spirit of Hernan Cortes and Bernal Diaz, until the worst of the anti-Catholic laws were withdrawn. In recent years the Mexican government has become less hostile to the Faith. Millions greeted Pope John Paul II when, on January 27, 1979, he became the first Pope to visit the shrine of Our Lady of Guadalupe and to behold directly the portrait of the Mother of God, to whom he has a very special devotion.

But Our Lady of Guadalupe is not only the "Happiness of Mexico."[137] Every well authenticated personal appearance of the Mother of God in history is immensely significant to the whole world. No more than it could be a coincidence that there were five million Indian baptisms in Mexico in the first five years after she appeared on the hill of Tepeyac, can it be a coincidence that those five same years, 1532-1536, were the years that England left the Catholic Church. In April 1532, just five months after the apparition, the clergy of England formally submitted to the authority of

Henry VIII, who was demanding an annulment of his marriage to Catherine of Aragon–Queen Isabel's youngest daughter–which Pope Clement VIII had refused, on the best of grounds, to grant. The next month St. Thomas More resigned as Chancellor of England because his king was moving into rebellion against the Church Christ founded. In May 1533 Thomas Cranmer, Henry VIII's choice as Archbishop of Canterbury (the highest ecclesiastical office in England), recognized Henry's marriage to Anne Boleyn, and in July Pope Clement excommunicated the King of England. In March 1534 Parliament declared the final severance of the Church of England from the Roman Catholic Church, and ordered all its members, clergymen and public officials to take an oath recognizing the legitimacy of the King's marriage despite the declaration of the Pope. St. Thomas More refused to take this oath. In November 1534 Parliament passed the Act of Supremacy making Henry VIII supreme head of the Church in England. The clergy were required to take an oath accepting that as well; only one bishop, St. John Fisher, refused. He was martyred for it on June 22, 1535; St. Thomas More was martyred July 6, 1535. In April 1536 Parliament and king, prodded by the rapacious Thomas Cromwell, expropriated the land and all the property of every monastery in England.

The parallel is breathtakingly precise, diamond-clear. As the people of England went out of the Church Christ founded, the people of Mexico came into it. The consequences to the Church of the loss of England reverberate down the centuries; she has suffered few greater losses in the whole of the Christian era. The consequences to the Church of the conversion of the majority of the population of the New World who live south of the United States still lie mostly in the future. But no part of the world is more Catholic, and few equally so–and that is, above all, the gift of the Virgin of Guadalupe.

Afterword

On the 31ˢᵗ day of July in the Year of Our Lord 2002 His Holiness Pope John Paul II presided over the canonization of Juan Diego Cuauhtlatoatzin at the Basilica of Our Lady of Guadalupe in Mexico City.

Juan Diego is the first Native American canonized by the Catholic Church. Despite the objections of many critics, there is solid historical evidence and documentation of both his existence and his holiness.

The original manuscript account of the apparition of Our Lady of Guadalupe was actually found in the New York Public Library. Critical editions of the basic Guadalupan documents, both Aztec and Spanish, have been published. They refer to a Marian apparition that actually took place at a particular time and in a specified place. The most ancient of these goes back to the year 1537 and comes from the city of Colima in Mexico. We know that the first shrine to Our Lady of Guadalupe was actually built by Bishop Zumarraga at Tepeyac, and frequently visited by the people of Mexico City.

A Mexican Indian named Gabriel Suarez testified in a formal hearing in 1666 at the age of 110 that his father had known Juan Diego well, had seen the sacred portrait of Our Lady of Guadalupe and knew many people who had gone to Juan Diego's home to ask him to pray for them.

Juan Diego may serve for us today, as he did in his own time, as a representative of his people to whom the Blessed Virgin Mary came to bring her Son. She also brought the unforgettable, hauntingly beautiful, and miraculous portrait of herself, as she actually appeared, as Christ Himself saw her and as she is in Heaven today, to which she was gloriously assumed. That portrait remains brilliantly visible in her present day basilica, successor to the one which she asked Juan Diego to tell Bishop Zumarraga to build for her. It is his monument for the ages, just as much as it is hers. He is her messenger forever, just like the children of Fatima. Now we know that he is gloriously reunited with her in Heaven.

Endnotes

1. R.C. Padden, *The Hummingbird and the Hawk* (New York, 1970), p.74.
2. Ibid., p. 39.
3. Ibid., p. 71.
4. Ibid., pp. 72-73.
5. Quoted in Salvador de Madariaga, *Hernan Cortes, Conqueror of Mexico* (Chicago, 1955), pp. 19-20.
6. *The Bernal Diaz Chronicles*, tr. & ed. Albert Idell (New York, 1956), p. 17
7. *Bernal Diaz Chronicles*, as translated by de Madariaga, *Cortes*, p. 74.
8. *Bernal Diaz Chronicles*, tr. Idell, p. 20.
9. Quoted in de Madariaga, Cortes, p. 77.
10. *Bernal Diaz Chronicles*, tr. Idell, pp. 28-29.
11. Ibid., p. 34.
12. Madariaga, *Cortes*, p. 95.
13. *Bernal Diaz Chronicles* as translated by de Madariaga, Cortes, pp. 103-104, and by Maurice Keatinge (New York, 1927), II, 529.
14. *Bernal Diaz Chronicles* as translated by de Madariaga, *Cortes*, p. 97.
15. *Bernal Diaz Chronicles*, tr. Idell, p. 52.
16. Miguel Leon-Portilla, ed., *The Broken Spears: The Aztec Account of the Conquest of Mexico* (Boston, 1962), pp. 23, 29.
17. Ibid., pp. 26, 28.
18. Ibid., p. 28.
19. Ibid.
20. Ibid.
21. Ibid., pp. 30-31.
22. *Bernal Diaz Chronicles*, tr. Idell, p. 60.
23. Ibid.
24. Ibid.
25. Ibid., pp. 60-61.
26. Ibid., p. 72.
27. Hernan Cortes, *Letters from Mexico*, tr. & ed. A. R. Pagden (New York, 1971), p. 35.
28. Ibid., p. 50.
29. *Bernal Diaz Chronicles*, tr. Idell, p. 88 (put in direct address).
30. *Bernal Diaz Chronicles* as translated by de Madariaga, *Cortes*, p. 232.
31. *Bernal Diaz Chronicles*, tr. Idell, p. 91.
32. Ibid., p. 93.
33. Ibid.
34. Ibid.
35. *Bernal Diaz Chronicles* as translated by de Madariaga, *Cortes*, p. 170.
36. *Bernal Diaz Chronicles*, tr. Idell, p. 96.
37. Ibid., p. 104.
38. *Cortes, Letters from Mexico*, p. 63.
39. Francisco Lopez de Gomara, *Cortes, the Life of the Conqueror*, tr. & ed. Lesley Byrd Simpson (Berkeley, Ca., 1964), p. 114.
40. *Bernal Diaz Chronicles*, tr. Idell, p. 109.
41. *Bernal Diaz Chronicles*, tr. Keatinge, II, 532.
42. Cortes, *Letters from Mexico*, p. 75.
43. *Bernal Diaz Chronicles*, tr. Idell, p. 135.
44. Leon-Portilla, ed., *Broken Spears*, p. 41.

45. Ibid., p. 55.
46. Madariaga, *Cortes*, pp. 222-223.
47. Ibid., p. 226.
48. *Bernal Diaz Chronicles*, tr. Idell, p. 138.
49. Madariaga, *Cortes*, p. 239.
50. Leon-Portilla, ed., *Broken Spears*, p. 64.
51. *Bernal Diaz Chronicles*, tr. Idell, p. 153.
52. Madariaga, *Cortes*, p. 99.
53. The title of C. Harvey Gardiner's biography of Sandoval (Carbondale, Ill., 1961).
54. *Bernal Diaz Chronicles*, tr. Keatinge, II, 530.
55. *Bernal Diaz Chronicles*, tr. Idell, p. 147.
56. Ibid.
56. Ibid., p. 197.
58. A moment of confusion in Bernal Diaz's usually accurate memory has caused many writers to assume that the temple the Spaniards visited on this day was that of Tlatelolco, the northern suburb of Mexico City, rather than the great temple dedicated in 1487. Padden, *Hummingbird and Hawk*, p. 291, proves that it must have been the great temple that they visited.
59. For the ossuary see Gormara, *Cortes*, p. 167, and Andres de Tapia's account in Patricia de Fuentes, ed., *The Conquistadors: First-Person Accounts of the Conquest of Mexico* (New York, 1963), pp. 41-42.
60. Madariaga, *Cortes*, p. 250.
61. *Bernal Diaz Chronicles* as translated by de Madariaga, Cortes, pp. 253-254.
62. Ibid., p. 254.
63. Maurice Collis, Cortes and Montezuma (New York, 1954), p. 135.
64. *Bernal Diaz Chronicles*, tr. Idell, p. 170.
65. Ibid., p. 178.
66. Ibid., pp. 193-194.
67. Padden, *Hummingbird and Hawk*, p. 185.
68. Madariaga, *Cortes*, p. 291.
69. Ibid., p. 292.
70. *Bernal Diaz Chronicles* as translated by de Madariaga, *Cortes,* p. 295.
71. Cortes, *Letters from Mexico*, p. 107.
72. Gomara, *Cortes* p. 190.
73. Collis, *Cortes and Montezuma*, p. 176.
74. Ibid.
75. Leon-Portilla, ed., *Broken Spears*, p. 72.
76. Cortes, *Letters from Mexico*, p. 130.
77. *Bernal Diaz Chronicles*, tr. Idell, p. 247.
78. Ibid., p. 251.
79. Ibid., p. 252.
80. Fuentes, ed., *Conquistadors*, p. 155.
81. Cortes, *Letters from Mexico*, p. 142.
82. Fuentes, ed., *Conquistadors*, p. 142.
83. *Bernal Diaz Chronicles,* tr. Idell, pp. 257-258.
84. Ibid., p. 258.
85. Ibid., p. 393.
86. Ibid., p. 258.
87. Ibid., p. 261.
88. Cortes, *Letters from Mexico*, p. 169.
89. *Bernal Diaz Chronicles*, tr. Idell. pp. 294-295.
90. Ibid., p. 326.

91. Ibid., p. 333.
92. Cortes, *Letters from Mexico*, p. 223.
93. Burr C. Brundage, *A Rain of Darts: The Mexica Aztecs* (Austin, Tx.,1 9 7 2), pp. 285-286.
94. Cortes, *Letters from Mexico*, p. 245.
95. *Bernal Diaz Chronicles*, tr. Idell, p. 387.
96. Cortes, *Letters from Mexico*, p. 239.
97. *Bernal Diaz Chronicles*, tr. Idell, p. 379.
98. Ibid., p. 383.
99. Ibid., p. 384.
100. See Note 55, above.
101. See Note 13, above.
102. *Bernal Diaz Chronicles*, tr. Keatinge, II, 545-546.
103. Ibid., II, 548.
104. Leon-Portilla, ed., *Broken Spears*, p. 51.
105. Madariaga, *Cortes*, p. 427.
106. Ibid., p. 428.
107. Robert Ricard, *The Spiritual Conquest of Mexico* (Berkeley, Ca., 1966), p. 86.
108. Madariaga, *Cortes*, p. 431.
109. Cortes, *Letters from Mexico*, pp. 433-434.
110. Fidel J. Chauvet, "Fray Juan de Zumarraga, Protector of the Indians," *Americas* V (1948-49), 286-287.
111. Donald E. Chipman, *Nuno de Guzman and the Province of Panuco in New Spain*, 1518-1533 (Glendale, Ca., 1967), p. 170.
112. Madariaga, *Cortes*, p. 458.
113. Chipman, *Guzman and the Province of Panuco*, p. 236.
114. Ernest J. Burrus, S.J., *"The Oldest Copy of the Nican Mopohua,"* and "The Basic Bibliography of the Guadalupan Apparitions (1531-1723)," *CARA Studies on Popular Devotion, Volume IV: Guadalupan Studies*, No. 4 (Washington, D.C., 1981) and No. 5 (Washington, D.C., 1983).
115. William Thomas Walsh, *Our Lady of Fatima* (New York, 1947, 1954), p. 51.
116. *Nican Mopohua* of Antonio Valeriano, as translated in Charles J. Wahlig, *Past, Present and Future of Juan Diego* (Kenosha, Wis., 1972), p. 79.
117. Ibid.
118. Ibid., p. 81.
119. Ibid.
120. Ibid., p. 84.
121. Ibid., p. 83.
122. Ibid., p. 86.
123. Philip S. Callahan, "The Tilma under Infra-Red Radiation," *CARA Studies of Popular Devotion, Volume II: Guadalupan Studies*, No. 3 (Washington, 1981), pp. 9-10.
124. Ibid., pp. 10-11.
125. Ibid., pp. 14-15.
126. Wahlig, *Juan Diego*, pp. 122-124 and Appendix.
127. Letter of Bishop Zumarraga to Cortes, dated (by internal evidence) December 24, 1531, in P. Mariano Cuevas, *Historia de la Iglesia en Mexico* (El Paso, Tx., 1928), I, 282; translation by Warren H. Carroll.
128. Ricard, *Spiritual Conquest of Mexico*, p. 91.
129. T. R. Fehrenbach, *Fire and Blood: A History of Mexico* (New York, 1951), p. 209.
130. Charles Gibson, *Tlaxcala in the Sixteenth Century* (New Haven, Ct., 1952), pp. 37-38.
131. Ricard, *Spiritual Conquest of Mexico*, p. 101.

132. This is shown in material that was complied and displayed by Msgr. Enrique Salazar, postulator for the cause of the canonization of Juan Diego by the Catholic Church, which took place on July 31, 2002.

133. Donald Demarest and Coley Taylor, *The Dark Virgin: The Book of Our Lady of Guadalupe* (New York, 1956), p. 169.

134. Ibid., pp. 170-171.

135. Herbert F. Leies, *Mother of a New World: Our Lady of Guadalupe* (Westminster, Md., 1964), p. 161.

136. See Note 120 above.

137. Title of Luis Becerra Tarco's famous book about Our Lady Guadalupe, published in Mexico City in 1675.

Bibliography

Ascensio, Luis Medina, S.J. "The Apparitions of Guadalupe as Historical Events," *CARA Studies on Popular Devotion*, Volume II: *Guadalupan Studies*, No. 1. Washington, 1979.

Bancroft, Hubert H. *History of Mexico*, Volume II (1521-1600). San Francisco, 1883.

Brundage, Burr C. *A Rain of Darts: The Mexican Aztecs*. Austin, Tx., 1972.

Burland, C.A. *The Gods of Mexico*. London, 1967.

_____. *Montezuma, Lord of the Aztecs*. London, 1973.

Burrus, Ernest J., S.J. "The Basic Bibliography of the Guadalupan Apparitions," *CARA Studies on Popular Devotion*, Volume IV: *Guadalupan Studies, No. 5*. Washington, 1983.

_____. "The Oldest Copy of the *Nican Mopohua*," *CARA Studies on Popular Devotion*, Volume IV: *Guadalupan Studies, No. 4*. Washington, 1981.

Carroll, Warren H. *The Cleaving of Christendom*. A History of Christendom, Vol. 4. Front Royal, Virginia: Christendom Press, 2000.

_____. *Isabel of Spain: The Catholic Queen*. Front Royal, Virginia: Christendom Press, 1991.

Cassidy, Joseph L. *Mexico, Land of Mary's Wonders*. Paterson, N.J., 1958.

Castaneda, Carlos E. "Fray Juan de Zumarraga and Indian Policy in New Spain," *Americas* V (1948-1949), 296-310.

Chauvet, Fidel de J. "Fray Juan de Zumarraga, Protector of the Indians," *Americas* V (1948-49), 283-295.

Chipman, Donald E. *Nuno de Guzman and the Province of Panuci in New Spain, 1518-1533*. Glendale, Ca., 1967.

Collis, Maurice. *Cortes and Montezuma*. New York, 1954.

Cortes, Hernan. *Letters from Mexico*, ed., A. R. Pagden. New York, 1971.

Cuevas, P. Mariano, S.J. *Historia de la Iglesia en Mexico*, Volume I. El Paso, Tx., 1928.

Demarest, Donald and Coley Taylor. *The Dark Virgin: The Book of Our Lady of Guadalupe*. New York, 1956.

Diaz, Bernal. *The Bernal Diaz Chronicles: The True Story of the Conquest of Mexico*, ed. Albert Idell. Garden City, N.Y., 1956.

_____. *The True History of the Conquest of Mexico*, ed. Maurice Keatinge, 2 vols. New York, 1927.

Fehrenbach, T. R. *Fire and Blood: A History of Mexico*. New York, 1973.

Fuentes, Patricia de, ed. *The Conquistadors: First-Person Accounts of the Conquest of Mexico*. New York, 1963.

Gardinar, C. Harvey. *The Constant Captain, Gonzalo de Sandoval.*
Carbondale, Ill., 1961.

Gibson, Charles. *Tlaxcala in the Sixteenth Century.* New Haven, 1952.

Gomara, Francisco Lopez de. *Cortes, The Life of the Conqueror*, ed. Lesley
Byrd Simpson. Berkeley, 1964.

Hanke, Lewis. "The Contribution of Bishop Juan de Zumarraga to Mexican
Culture," *Americas* V (1948-49), 275-282.

Johnston, Francis. *The Wonder of Guadalupe.* Rockford, Ill., 1981.

Kelly, John E. *Pedro de Alvarado, Conquistador.* Princeton, N.J. 1932.

Leies, Herbert F. *Mother for a New World: Our Lady of Guadalupe.*
Westminster, Md., 1964.

Leon-Portilla, Miguel, ed. *The Broken Spears; The Aztec Account of the
Conquest of Mexico.* Boston, 1962.

_____. *La Protohistoria Guadalupana.* Mexico, 1981.

Madariaga, Salvador de. *Hernan Cortes, Conqueror of Mexico.*
Chicago, 1955.

Magner, James A., "Fray Juan de Zumarrage: His Social Contributions,"
Americas V (1948-49), 264-274

Merriman, Roger B. *The Rise of the Spanish Empire in the Old World and
in the New*, Volume III: *The Emperor.* New York, 1967.

Ricard, Robert. *The Spiritual Conquest of Mexico: An Essay on the
Apostolate and the Evangelizing Methods of the Mendicant Orders
in New Spain, 1523-1572.* Berkeley, 1966.

Sejourne, Laurette. *Burning Water: Thought and Religion in Ancient
Mexico.* New York, 1960.

Vaillant, George C. *Aztecs of Mexico: Origin, Rise and Fall of the Aztec
Nation.* Garden City, N.Y., 1950.

Wahlig, C.J. *Past, Present and Future of Juan Diego.* Kenosha, Wis., 1972.

Walsh, William T. *Isabella of Spain, the Last Crusader.* New York, 1930.

117

See all that Christendom Press has to offer by looking
through our on-line catalog.
www.christendompress.com

Email us:
press@christendom.edu

Call toll free: (8:30-4:30 ET)
800-698-6649

Fax us anytime
540-636-2170

Write to us:
Christendom Press
134 Christendom Dr.
Front Royal, VA 22630